The Plant Kingdom

illustrated by Henry Barnet

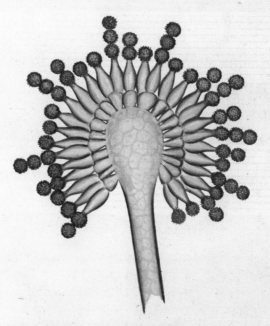

Hamlyn · London
Sun Books · Melbourne

FOREWORD

The aim of this book is to demonstrate two things: first, the range of plant structure throughout a group of at least 300,000 species; and second, how plants have tackled the same problems in a wide variety of ways. These two approaches are treated separately – the first in pages 10 to 67, and the second in pages 68 to 155.

Many scientific terms have been used deliberately throughout the book, but are fully explained. No apology is offered for this, nor for the fact that viruses, bacteria and even fungi are not plants – but neither are they animals. These three groups have been included to provide a contrast with the true plants and to illustrate more fully the complete range of complexity, from the smallest to the largest.

Plants have suffered from 'under-exposure'. Apart from the interest of gardeners, they have not been subjected to much public attention in comparison with the vast numbers of films and books devoted to wild animals. If human beings were themselves plants, the situation might well have been reversed. It is hoped that this little book may contribute something towards that end.   I.T.

The artist wishes to thank the members of the staff of the Library and Herbarium of the Royal Botanic Gardens at Kew, and the various departments of Botany at the British Museum, for their valuable help in providing pictorial references.

Published by The Hamlyn Publishing Group Limited
London · New York · Sydney · Toronto
Hamlyn House, Feltham, Middlesex, England
In association with Sun Books Pty Ltd Melbourne

SBN 600 00096 6

Phototypeset by Filmtype Services, Scarborough
Colour separations by Schwitter Limited, Zurich
Printed in England by Sir Joseph Causton & Sons Limited

CONTENTS

INTRODUCTION

'What is a plant?' is a simple question without a simple answer. It is easy to say that a plant is green, having stems, roots and leaves; that it does not move, and that each cell is surrounded by a wall of cellulose. Numerous exceptions can be found to all these points, however. First, not all plants are green – some are colourless and dependent on other living organisms for their food, while others appear brown, yellow or red, due to the presence of other pigments. Admittedly stems, roots and leaves are typical organs of the higher plants, such as those we cultivate, but even here the distinction may be somewhat arbitrary and sometimes misleading. In fact, these organs do not occur as such in lower plants where we can only refer to the flattened or lobed plant body as a thallus (seaweeds, liverworts) or to the white filamentous strands of fungi as a mycelium.

Again, while plants do not move on their roots, there are many plants which have one or more simple stages in their life where the plants can move about by whip-like structures known as flagella. Movement is also found in many leaves and in the animal-catching traps of carnivorous plants. Similarly, exceptions can also be found to the general feature of the plant cell wall in a number of simple plants where the cells are naked, or where the wall is not, as is generally supposed, composed principally of cellulose.

With these drawbacks to the definition of a plant in mind, we can say that true plants include algae, mosses and liverworts, ferns and their allies, conifers and flowering plants. Bacteria, fungi and viruses have many characters quite divorced from those of true plants. The fungi are nowadays often referred to as the Third Kingdom, as they are neither plants nor animals. However, they are probably closer to plants than to animals, and for this reason are included in this book. Viruses, on the other hand, are in dispute as to whether they can be called living at all.

1. Fly Agaric fungus 2. Maidenhair fern, *Adiantum capillus-veneris* 3. Liverwort, *Pellia epiphylla* 4. Lichen, *Leptogium* 5. Alga, *Ascophyllum nodosum* 6. Angiosperm, *Hawarthia margarantifera* 7. Gymnosperm, Giant Redwood, *Sequoia gigantea*

Evolution and classification

The existence of so many different types of plants and animals is due to the process of **evolution.** Although it is still far from understood, evolution is a result of **variation,** which is primarily due to **mutation** (alteration in some slight but specific way of the genetic material). Potentially, plants are capable of considerable variation, but most of this is suppressed by **natural selection** (survival of the fittest). On the other hand, natural selection may favour the mutant, which may succeed the original species or be separated from it. In this way, new species are slowly formed, with **extinction** of one species or another removing the direct link between them. It is the process of extinction over millions of years which makes whole groups of plants stand apart, so that it is difficult to understand how they are related. In human terms this can best be explained by 'the missing links'. We can surmise and prove, that we originated from some form of ape, yet the actual intermediary species are extinct; the apes with which we shared common ancestry have also evolved, so that it is impossible to find a living ape with which we have a direct affinity.

It is possible to systematically relate various plants and animals by a system of names **(taxonomy).** In this book both the latin and common names of plants are quoted; the use of common names is not always feasible, as many plants do not have them. All plants have, however, latin names which comprise two parts. The first, or generic name (single, **genus;** plural **genera**) is used to denote a number of plants which have close affinities. The second name, the name of the species, is one specific to that plant, and is, theoretically, the smallest unit in classification. A third name, that of a variety or strain, is sometimes added after the specific name. At the other end of the scale, a number of genera may be grouped together to form **tribes,** which together comprise a **family,** and so on. In this way, classification links plants together in a system which reflects their affinities, but more commonly is a convenient system for accurate recognition of a plant to avoid the confusion of common names. Common names can refer to quite different species; for example, in Britain the name Cowslip refers to *Primula veris,* while in the United States it is applied to *Caltha palustris,* known in Britain as the Marsh Marigold.

Terminology

Binary fission: a simple form of asexual multiplication which involves the splitting of a single cell into two daughter cells. This is a term applied to organisms which consist of a single cell (**unicellular**), and must not be confused with the cell division (**mitosis**) of **multicellular** organisms.

DNA, RNA: nucleic acids, the genetic material of the cell. In all organisms save some viruses, DNA is the master molecule, acting as the chemical blueprint for all the activities of the organism. DNA is mainly restricted to the **nucleus**, the dark staining structure embedded within the cytoplasm. The **cytoplasm** is the membranous bulk of the cell, containing numerous small structures with specialized functions.

Mycelium: a complex weft of colourless shrouds in the vegetative structure of fungi.

Nitrogen fixation: the process by which gaseous nitrogen is converted into useful solid compounds. This is an energy-requiring process, restricted to a few lower organisms.

Photosynthesis: essentially a light-driven process which converts atmospheric **carbon dioxide** (CO_2) into carbon compounds such as sugars. Light is harnessed into useful chemical energy by means of pigments, the most common of which is **chlorophyll,** responsible for the green colour of plants.

Respiration: the reverse of photosynthesis, whereby organic compounds are broken down to release carbon dioxide and energy, which can be used in other processes.

Rhizome: an underground stem. Common examples are found in Iris, Water Lily and Lilly of the Valley.

Sexual reproduction: the difference between this process and asexual reproduction is that sexual gametes are produced. In the case of higher plants the transfer of pollen (which contains the male gametes) to the female organs is known as **pollination,** and must occur before the fusion of the gametes takes place (**fertilization.**)

Thallus: usually a ribbon-like structure found in lower plant groups representing the main plant body.

Vacuole: most of the cell space in true plants is occupied by this structure, which comprises a membranous bag of fluid. In the rest of the cell there are usually numerous smaller vacuoles (**vesicles**) that contain various special compounds.

| pp 10-11 | | **VIRUSES**
RNA – viruses
DNA – viruses |

| pp 12-17 | | **BACTERIA**
True Bacteria
Myxobacteria
Spirochaetes
Blue-green Algae |

| pp 18-25 |  | **FUNGI**
Lower Fungi
Ascomycetes
Basidiomycetes
Myxomycetes |

| pp 26-27 | | **LICHENS**
Composite plants,
comprising an alga
and a fungus |

| pp 28-35 | | **ALGAE**
Orange and Yellow
Diatoms
Red
Brown
Green |

BRYOPHYTES
Liverworts – Thallose
Leafy
Mosses

pp 36-43

PTERIDOPHYTES
Psilophytes
Psilotes
Lycopods
Horsetails
True Ferns

pp 44-51

GYMNOSPERMS
Cycads
Ginkgos
Conifers (Pines)
Gnetales

pp 52-58

ANGIOSPERMS
Dicotyledons
Monocotyledons

pp 59-67

PLANT GROUPS

The viruses

Viruses are the simplest form of life known and show few of the properties of other living organisms. They do not breathe, feed, grow or move, and only become active when they invade a host to cause disease. Moreover, they can be crystallized in a similar manner to cooking salt, and stored under unfavourable conditions, such as high temperatures, without affecting their virulence.

As viruses pass through the finest of man-made filters, and can only be individually seen under the highest powers of the electron miscroscope, it is hardly surprising that those who first investigated viral diseases believed they were caused by a poisonous fluid. These unusual features are due to the fact that viruses are non-cellular, with no membranes, nucleus or other organelles.

However, in spite of their small size, any given virus has a precise structure, consisting of a protein coat, or shell, inside which is the nucleic acid which acts as a chemical blueprint for the activities of the organism. The protein coat usually comcomprises a number of identical units arranged rather as bricks are cemented together to form a house. The nucleic acid is either DNA or RNA, in contrast with other organisms, which always have both. DNA is found more commonly in viruses

(Below right) Tobacco Mosaic Virus and *(left)* model of a section showing nucleic acid as an internal spiral

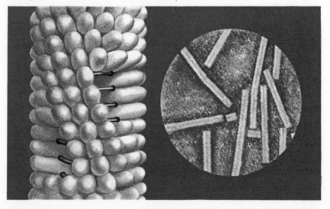

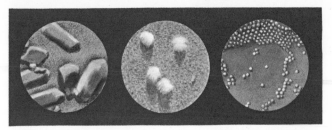

(Above from left to right) crystals of poliomyelitis virus, influenza virus and bushy stunt virus

which infect animals, and RNA in those which infect plants.

Bacteria are infected by viruses known as bacteriophages, which may be quite complex and comprise a head-piece containing DNA, a core, and a tail plate carrying fibres. A small passage connects the head-piece to the tail plate, and through this the DNA passes to the bacterium it is infecting. These viruses, when added to a culture of bacteria, cause a breakdown of the cells (lysis), and this can be seen as a series of grey, liquid spots, or plaques.

(Below) Bacteriophage T4 *(left)* and Lysis *(right)*

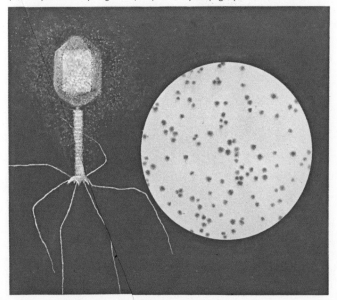

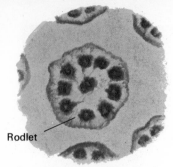

Rodlet

Internal structure of flagellum

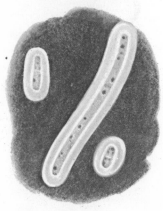

Escherichia coli

Bacillus megaterium

The bacteria

True bacteria are minute, usually unicellular organisms, many of which are responsible for disease. Although many are immobile, bacteria which have flagella can move by means of these small whips which lash to and fro. In section, each flagellum can be clearly seen to contain a number of strengthening rods arranged in a definite pattern.

The shape of true bacterial cells can be broadly classified into three types – rods; spheres (cocci); and spirals (spirilla). *Escherichia coli* is one of the coliform bacteria found in intestines. It is rod-shaped and surrounded by numerous fibres (not flagella). It can live with or without oxygen, although its presence in water is a sign of contamination by sewage.

Bacillus megaterium is another rod-shaped bacterium, which is unpigmented and surrounded by flagella. The cell walls are covered by a dense layer of protective mucilage, the capsule. Bacterial cell walls contain a number of distinctive chemicals, rendering the bacterium sensitive to several stains. Penicillin prevents the synthesis of cell walls, which accounts for its lethal effect on bacteria.

Pseudomonas fluorescens belongs to a large group of bacteria which can live on a wide variety of foods – as many as 100 kinds. It is a yellow-green bacterium with a pronounced sheen to its colonies in culture, and is commonly found in water and soil. Flagella are present only at one end of the cell.

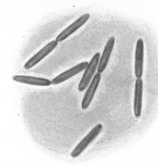

Pseudomonas flourescens

Thiospirillum belongs to the purple sulphur bacteria, one of the groups of photosynthetic bacteria. Yellow grains of sulphur are deposited in the large spiral cells, each of which bears flagella at one end. They are common in hot sulphur springs and in water where no oxygen is present. The green photosynthetic bacteria are very similar in their structure and behaviour.

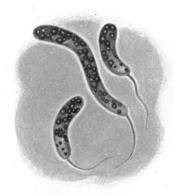

Thiospirillum

Nitrosomonas is able to convert ammonia to nitrite, thereby releasing energy to fix carbon dioxide. The cells are very small, with flagella attached to one end, and multiply by simple fission. The related *Nitrobacter* is also completely dependent on inorganic compounds, oxidizing nitrite to nitrate. Both organisms are therefore important in the nitrogen cycle.

Caulobacter – a member of an unusual group of stalked bacteria – has sausage-shaped

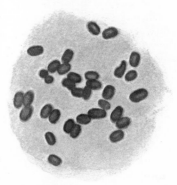

Nitrosomonas

cells with a stalk at one end. The stalks bear a disc at the tip which anchors the cell to its support. *Caulobacter* often forms small colonies of cells joined by their stalks. Multiplication occurs by simple division of the cells by a constriction about their middle (binary fission).

Rhodomicrobium, in contrast with the simple binary fission of *Caulobacter* and other bacteria, multiplies by budding. The parent cell slowly extrudes a daughter cell, which buds off to form a new cell; these remain attached to the parent cells, forming a very simple branched colony. In other respects, as its colour indicates, this bacterium is identical with the purple bacteria.

Streptomyces is a mycelial bacterium; that is, it is not unicellular but forms a much-branched filamentous structure, a mycelium. Like many fungi, special spores are produced in chains. However, their size and internal structure is akin to the bacteria, and quite distinct from the fungi. Many members of the *Streptomyces* group produce important antibiotics, including streptomycin, tetracycline and chloramphenicol.

Pleuropneumonia bacteria

Caulobacter

Rhodomicrobium

Streptomyces

Pleuropneumonia organism

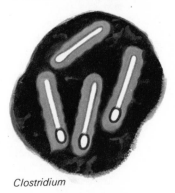

Clostridium

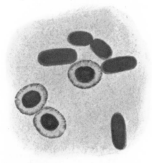

Azotobacter

have no rigid cell wall, and therefore easily change shape according to the medium in which they are growing. They are responsible for respiratory diseases in animals, including man. Under certain conditions true bacteria show the same plasticity, indicating that pleuropneumonia are bacteria which have lost the ability to form a normal cell wall.

Clostridium illustrates the problem of bacterial classification – there is relatively little morphological difference between bacteria, and they are thus distinguished to a great extent on their chemical characteristics. Thus, some species ferment cellulose, while others feed on amino acids, sugars, uric acid or acetic acid. All *Clostridium* species are, however, straight rods surrounded by flagella, and oxygen is lethal to them.

Azotobacter shares with green and purple bacteria, and blue-green algae, the ability to convert nitrogen from the atmosphere into useful compounds, such as amino acids. *Azotobacter* has an appearance that comprises paired rods surrounded by flagella, and produces spherical resting spores. All species require oxygen for their feeding on various chemicals.

15

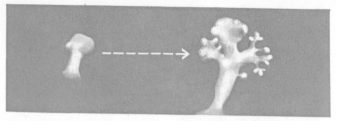

Development of fruiting *Chondromyces,* a myxobacterium

The myxobacteria

The differences between the true bacteria and the myxobacteria are concerned with the way in which they move and the flexibility of the cell wall. Bacteria move by flagella, but the myxobacteria have no comparable structure, and move by gliding in contact with solid surfaces. The cells, which appear much like the rods of some bacteria, remain independent of each other during growth, but at fruiting come together in a slime, producing a fruiting body of specialized cells, which is often brightly coloured.

The spirochaetes

The structure of the spirochaetes shows some unusual features. The cells may be described as long flexible cylinders, which have an external elastic filament anchored at both ends. This causes the cells to be wound in a helix; this helix disappears if the elastic filament is removed by enzymes. Spirochaetes are aquatic and responsible for many serious diseases. In man, they cause illnesses such as jaundice and fever.

(Below) illustrations of how tension exerted by an axial filament causes twisting in the spirochaetes

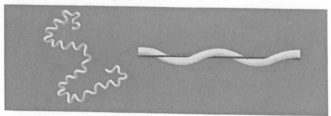

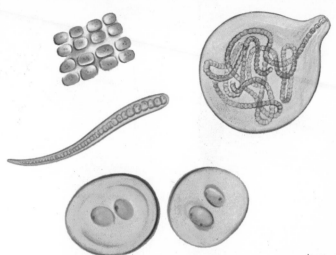

A selection of blue-green algae

The blue-green algae

This class of organisms is incorrectly named. Although they often appear blue-green in colour, they are almost certainly not algae, as their structure and chemical composition are more similar to that of the bacteria than that of the algae. In common with the bacteria and their allied forms, they have no true nucleus. The cells, which are rod-shaped or spherical, are found either singly or in strands, and are sheathed in a slime, enabling some unicellular kinds to form loose colonies. The bright colours of the blue-green algae seen under the microscope are caused by pigments present both in this slime sheath and in the cells themselves, where they play a vital part in the manufacture of food.

In common with Myxobacteria, the cells are able to glide over solid surfaces, but the mechanism by which they do this is not yet known, as they have no visible means of movement. These organisms are found in open water, where they constitute an important part of the plankton, and in hot springs, where few other organisms can exist. They also occur in soils, forming a greenish slime on the surface, or inhabit minute crevices in rocks and stones.

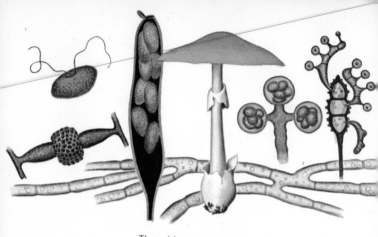

The wide range of structures in the fungi group

The fungi

The fungi have a number of features which place them in a separate category from true plants. They have no chlorophyll and cannot therefore use the sun's energy to make their own food. Their structure is a mycelium composed of numerous minute filaments, or hyphae, branching in all directions; the individual hyphae may consist of one or more cells, and are shown in the picture above. In the fruiting body, best seen in the form of a mushroom or toadstool, these hyphae are closely packed, and may contain a number of bright pigments. Their cell walls often contain chitin, a chemical found in animals, and cellulose, a normal component of true plant cell walls.

The lower fungi

These are extremely varied in their structure and reproduction, though a feature they share in common is the simplicity of their fruiting bodies. Asexual spores are produced mainly in sporangia, as can be seen in the case of *Rhizopus,* a common mould found on stale bread. The rounded black sporangia are produced at the tips of upright specialized hyphae, known as sporangiophores.

Each spore when liberated produces a new mycelium if it lands on a suitable source of food, and in turn produces its own spores. In the case of *Plasmopara viticola,* the tips of the branched sporangiophore are budded off to give detachable spores. The spores of *Entomophthora muscae,* a fungus which lives on flies, are also produced by budding at the tip of a bulbous hypha. One interesting difference, however, lies in the way in which the building and discharge of the spore occur; the budding process results in the ejection of the spore to some distance away from the parent hypha.

Sexual spores are produced directly from the cell which results from the fusion of the gametes; this cell produces a hardened coat which enables it to exist under severe conditions, and is in some cases known as a zygospore.

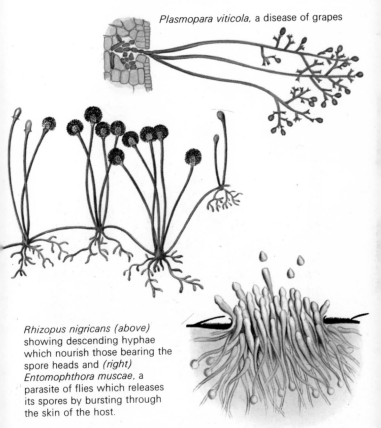

Plasmopara viticola, a disease of grapes

Rhizopus nigricans (above) showing descending hyphae which nourish those bearing the spore heads and *(right) Entomophthora muscae,* a parasite of flies which releases its spores by bursting through the skin of the host.

19

The ascomycetes

These are characterized by the presence of a special structure known as an ascus, within which the sexual spores, or ascospores, are produced. The asci are contained within a fruiting body, or ascocarp, whose structure enables these fungi to be further classified. Some of the variety of these ascocarps is shown in the accompanying illustrations of *Morchella*, *Ceratocystis* and *Sarcosoma*. *Morchella* species, known as the morels or sponge mushrooms, have an ascocarp which consists of a stalk and a cap which is delicately ridged. The asci are produced on the cap, and open by means of a hinged lid. All the morels are edible and are much prized as a delicacy.

The gelatinous ascocarps of *Sarcosoma* may reach a size of 2 inches in diameter, and the asci are produced on the inner surface of the cup. In both these types of fungi, therefore, the asci are exposed, but in *Ceratocystis* they are formed within the bulbous base of the ascocarp. The slender neck of the ascocarp is several times as long as the base, and each ascospore is released through the tip of this neck in a slimy droplet.

(Below left) Ceratocystis fimbriata, (right) the mould, Aspergillus niger

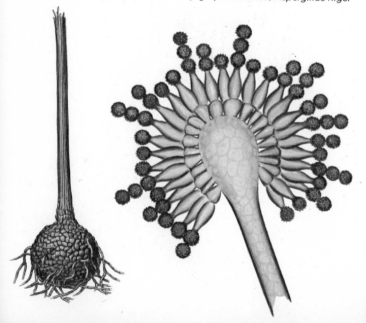

Sarcosoma globosum

The morel, *Morchella esculenta*

Asexual spores are usually produced in chains at the tips of specialized hyphae, and one of the best examples of this is *Aspergillus*. Here, the spore chains are produced all over the tip of the hypha. *Aspergillus* is another contaminant of bread, but can also be found growing on a wide variety of foods and materials. The white moulds sometimes found on leather may be caused by this fungus, and because of its ability to feed on so many substances, it is now used industrially in fermenting and the production of many chemicals. It is also known to cause lung and ear diseases in many animals, including man.

Another class of Ascomycetes which is very important includes the yeasts. These normally multiply asexually by budding, as they are unicellular, but a simple form of mycelium is sometimes found under certain conditions of culture. Some species produce asci, though not in an ascocarp.

The value of the yeasts in baking and fermenting is well known and this is a result of their ability to break down sugar into alcohol and carbon dioxide. The related leaf-curl fungi are responsible for many diseases of higher plants, for example, the 'witches broom' found on cherries.

The basidiomycetes

This group includes mushrooms and toadstools, bracket (or shelf) fungi, rusts and smuts, many of which are economically important, as in the case of Dry Rot. They are the most complex of the fungi, and the sexual spores are produced at the tips of bulbous hyphae, which in many cases form 'gills', as seen in the edible mushroom. In other cases, these special hyphae, called basidia (from which these fungi derive their name), are enclosed in the fruiting body, and the spores are only liberated by rupture or decay of the surrounding tissue, or by special discharge mechanisms.

Many basidiomycetes, such as mushrooms and toadstools, are only visible at certain times of the year, when the fruiting bodies (basidiocarps) grow very rapidly from the mycelium, which feeds on decaying wood or lives in association with the roots of nearby trees. Other forms have fruiting bodies which may last through the year, while many bracket fungi, such as

1. *Clavicorona pyxidata*
2. A shelf fungus, *Grifola sulphurea*

3. Dry-rot fungus, *Merulius lacrymans*

Polyporus sulphureus, produce additional portions to the existing basidiocarp each year. *Calocera* grows on dead wood, and produces its basidiocarps from the mycelium embedded within the wood. It is very waxy in its appearance and is one of the so-called jelly fungi.

The rusts and smuts are very specialized parasites of higher plants, often involving two hosts in their life-cycle. The rusts which infect cereals are perhaps the best known: the fungus completes several stages of its life on a cereal plant during the summer, and then over-winters on a perennial such as the Barberry, which acts as a source of infection the following year. One of the methods of control of this disease, therefore, has been the destruction of the second host plant.

An example of a basidiomycete in which the spores are initially buried is *Geastrum,* one of the earthstar puffballs. The basidiocarp is produced as a rough ball above the leaf litter in woodland, and splits open to reveal an inner layer through the

4. Earthstar, *Geastrum fimbriatum*

5. *Cyathus striatus*
6. *Calocera cornea*

top of which the spores escape. The coral fungi, whose appearance explains their popular name, may be represented by *Clavicorona pyxidata,* which is found growing among leaf litter. Among the most beautiful of the fungi, the coral fungi are coloured in shades of violet, orange or yellow. *Cyathus* is one of the most unusual fungi, as its spores are produced in little cups which play an important part in spore release.

The myxomycetes

These organisms, the slime moulds, were at one time thought to be animals, the reason for this being that they are capable of movement, and can travel some distance over soil, lawns and shrubs. However, their fruiting bodies are distinctly plant-like in structure and contain substances only found in the plant kingdom. The fruiting bodies produce spores which are extremely resistant to drought, and can survive for many years under conditions lethal to practically all other organisms – one example is where spores germinated after collection from a specimen that had been dry for over sixty years. The germinating spore releases swarm cells which move by flagella, as in the case of *Reticularia lycoperdon.* These swarmers fuse sexually, giving rise to a single cell which enlarges until it reaches a size which may be several feet in diameter. This slime-like structure is known as a plasmodium, and is the mobile stage. It

Reticularia swarm cell (×2000) and *(right) Ceratiomyxa fruticulosa* (×20)

24

moves by a contraction process, rather like an *Amoeba*. Under the microscope, the cell contents can be seen to be rapidly streaming in one direction and then another. The colours of these plasmodia are very varied and striking, including white, green, blue, violet, orange, red and yellow. The organism may overwinter by the conversion of the plasmodium into a hardened structure, which once again becomes a slime under warmer conditions. Eventually, however, the plasmodium will become a fruiting body and produce its spores, either in separate sporangia (of which *Hemitrichia stipitata* is an example), in groups of fused sporangia, or in a fused structure which has the same shape as the plasmodium. *Physarum,* widely distributed in America and tropical countries, produces a branched fruiting body raised on stalks above the original plasmodium, and coated in lime. Some of the patterns of the sporangial coats are quite intricate and delicate, and are often brightly coloured. *Ceratiomyxa* is unusual in that the fruiting body is covered in hairs, many of which bear spores; each spore represents a single sporangium in which the sporangial and spore coats are fused. The myxomycetes are of little economic importance, although the plasmodia may be of some use as they seed on minute organisms in the soil, engulfing their food rather in the manner of *Amoeba*. The colour of their plasmodia may in fact be enhanced by feeding on pigmented bacteria.

Hemitrichia vesporum (×20) and (right) *Physarum viride* (×20)

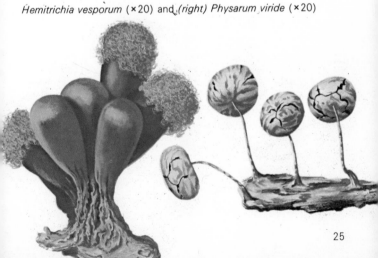

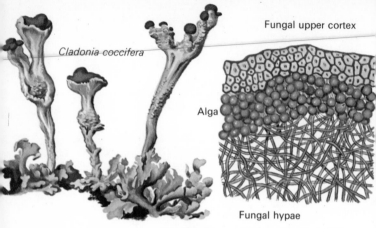

Fungal upper cortex

Cladonia coccifera

Alga

Fungal hypae

Magnified cross-section of a simple lichen

The lichens

The orange or grey-green plants which are very commonly seen as small brittle encrustations on old walls or stonework are lichens. There are several hundred known lichens, varying in shape and colour from white stalked forms to creeping black fronds. However varied they are, they share one feature in common: they are all 'composite' plants, a mixture of fungus and alga.

In the magnified cross-section of a simple lichen, the algal and fungal cells can easily be distinguished, as the alga tends to form a separate layer within the fungal hyphae. The outside of the lichen is composed of specialized fungal cells which help to prevent water loss, while the lower hyphae anchor the lichen to its support. In many cases, however, the algal and fungal cells are mixed together, and in other cases several additional layers are present.

The growth of a lichen is usually a few millimetres each decade. Lichens exist under difficult conditions, and the fungus, lacking chlorophyll to make its own food, feeds on the alga; in return, the alga receives protection from wind and loss of water. This means that as a lichen both components are able to grow where neither could on its own. For this reason, lichens are important colonizers of bare rock surfaces where few organisms can live; as they grow and die, so organic material is accumulated, and the growth of the lichen tends to break down the surface of the rock, making it possible for other plants, such as mosses, to grow.

Lichens are found in a wide variety of habitats – some are found by the seashore, covering the rocks on the upper shore away from the tides, others occur in the tundra of Arctic climates and form an important food for herbivores ('Reindeer moss'). More commonly, they are found on old walls, and buildings, in woods and on damp moors and heaths.

One of the most common groups of lichen is *Cladonia,* which is usually grey-green in colour and contrasts with the striking colour of its fruiting body, which is often red or orange. The fruiting body produced by the fungus usually contains asci and has a wide variety of shapes, as seen in *Lecidea, Thamnolia* and *Catillaria.*

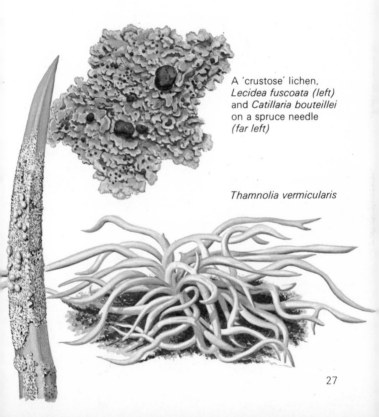

A 'crustose' lichen, *Lecidea fuscoata* (left) and *Catillaria bouteillei* on a spruce needle *(far left)*

Thamnolia vermicularis

The algae

The algae have already been mentioned in connection with the lichens; they are the simplest of the true plants, and can manufacture their own food by means of pigments which trap the sunlight. These pigments are very varied, but all algae contain the green chlorophylls of higher plants.

The predominant colour of an alga may also be red, brown, yellow or orange, due to the 'masking' of the green pigments by others. The algae are divided into several major groups on the basis of their colour, and this almost always also conforms with their structure and with their life-history.

The following main groups of algae are therefore recognized. These are brown algae, red algae, green algae, and stoneworts, and there is also a variety of unicellular and colonial forms, including the diatoms and related species.

Diatoms: a few examples of the multiplicity of forms

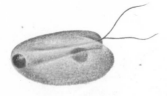

Peridinium

Cryptomonas anomala

The diatoms

Diatoms are unicellular algae whose cell walls have a very high percentage of silica. This silica shell is composed of two parts, one of which is slightly larger and overlaps the other. The exterior is etched in a wide variety of patterns which are often very intricate. Part of the living cytoplasm extrudes through the cell wall as a *raphe*, a thin filament which enables the diatom to move. Diatoms form a considerable portion of the plankton found at the surface of lakes and seas; they are also found on salt marshes.

Another type of unicellular alga found as plankton in both sea and fresh water is *Peridinium*. The cell wall is armoured, with a number of peculiar grooves running round it. In *Cryptomonas*, the flagella project from the front of the cell, from the top of a deep groove. Colonies of *Botryococcus* are sometimes found as a scum on the surface of ponds and lakes. The individual cells are joined into small colonies by a mucilage slime which they secrete. *Hydrurus* appears similar to many filamentous algae, although, like *Botryococcus,* its simple branched strands are enclosed in mucilage.

Hydrurus foetidus

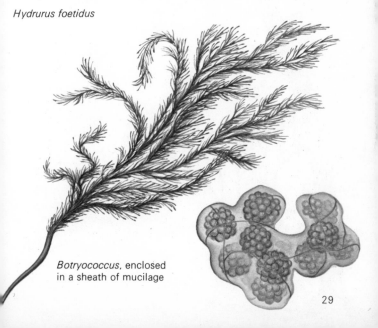

Botryococcus, enclosed in a sheath of mucilage

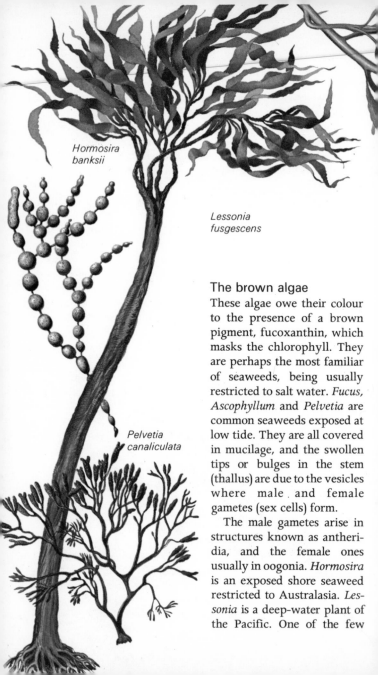

Hormosira banksii

Lessonia fusgescens

Pelvetia canaliculata

The brown algae

These algae owe their colour to the presence of a brown pigment, fucoxanthin, which masks the chlorophyll. They are perhaps the most familiar of seaweeds, being usually restricted to salt water. *Fucus, Ascophyllum* and *Pelvetia* are common seaweeds exposed at low tide. They are all covered in mucilage, and the swollen tips or bulges in the stem (thallus) are due to the vesicles where male and female gametes (sex cells) form.

The male gametes arise in structures known as antheridia, and the female ones usually in oogonia. *Hormosira* is an exposed shore seaweed restricted to Australasia. *Lessonia* is a deep-water plant of the Pacific. One of the few

Sargassum, *Sargasso filipendula*

forms that floats on the water is Sargassum which forms large masses such as the Sargasso Sea of the Mid-Atlantic.

In common with other groups of organisms, the algae have a sexual phase in their life-history, in which male and female gametes are produced in sexual organs, followed by fusion to form the zygote of a new generation. This process involves the fusion of genetic material (DNA) which in most organisms occurs as chromosomes within the nucleus.

Each event of sexual fusion would double the chromosome number in each successive generation were it not that during the formation of gametes the number of chromosomes is halved. If the halved (or haploid) number of chromosomes is represented by x, the sexual cycle can be thus symbolized:

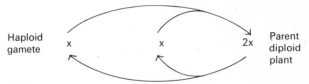

Haploid gamete x — x — $2x$ — Parent diploid plant

In lower organisms, and including many of the algae, the haploid (x) state is restricted to gametes, but in other organisms, the haploid condition exists as a separate plant. There is, therefore, an alternation of plants which are either haploid or diploid ($2x$). This is called the alternation of generations.

Laurencia papillosa

Corallina officinalis

Delesseria sanguinea

Batrachospermum moniliforme

The red algae

Red coloured algae owe their colour to the presence of the red pigment phycoerythrin. Perhaps the most spectacular species is *Delesseria sanguinea* which is almost fluorescent in its appearance. The thallus consists of a stem which produces thin fronds that look like leaves.

The cells of some other species such as *Chondria coerulescens* contain structures which make the plants iridescent. The violet fronds of *Batrachospermum* grow in freshwater streams attached to rocks. The stems are composed of numerous strands which give rise to whorls of branched filaments, and give the plant its characteristic appearance. *Porphyra* is a seaweed which has a broad, wavy thallus only a few cells thick.

A similar plant is *Gigartina,* whose surface is covered by minute warts, and which is anchored by a disc-shaped holdfast. The holdfast is a feature peculiar to the algae, comprising numerous thick rhizoids which bind the plants to rocks, sand, other seaweeds or animals. On some of the larger brown algae, these holdfasts are immense, and represent a very specialized form of tissue.

Another shape of growth common to all the major groups of algae is that shown by *Nemalion,* which is a marine summer annual. It has worm-like branches anchored by a holdfast. The jointed stems of *Corallina,* an inhabitant of rock pools and underwater ledges, are covered in lime, which the plant secretes. This tends to give it a pinkish appearance. The stems are tough and brittle. It is a relatively small plant, rarely exceeding 2 to 2½ inches in length. The greatest size to which red algae grow is about 3 feet, in contrast with the 100 feet achieved by some brown algae. *Laurencia* is another inhabitant of rock pools, having tubercular dark red stems. Species of *Janczewskia,* related to *Laurencia,* are parasitic on it, producing special invading structures which absorb the cell contents of the host.

Many red algae are a valuable source of complex sugars. Pectin is obtained commercially from algae, as is Carragheen. It is well known that seaweeds represent one of the commercial sources of iodine, and some species of the red algae contain cells very rich in this element. These algae also have the most complex and varied life-histories of the algal groups.

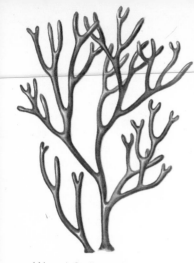

The green algae

These algae present a tremendous variety of forms, from unicells to complex thalloid types, though none approach the size reached by many of the brown algae. The green film found on many tree barks is often due to *Pleurococcus,* a simple unicellular alga. Another unicell is *Chlorella,* which is found in ponds and lakes.

A related alga is *Trentepohlia,* occasionally found in damp regions on walls and trees. Although *Trentepohlia montis-tabulae* is bright red-orange in colour, some of the other species of this genus are green. The alga grows as a prostrate filament which produces upright strands. These strands are topped by a peculiar cap the function of which is unknown. It is thought that *Trentepohlia* is an indicator of atmospheric pollution, as it is very sensitive to gases that are produced by combustion.

The membranous, bright green seaweeds belong to either *Ulva* or *Enteromorpha.* The thallus is extremely simple, and in *Ulva* is quite broad, while that of *Enteromorpha intestinalis* is tubular. *Ulva* is rather like a green version of *Porphyra,* the red

(Above) Codium tomentosum and *(below) Ulva lactuca*

alga, and it produces two generations which are identical; the haploid and diploid plants can only be distinguished by examining the cells under a microscope to count the chromosomes.

Codium is another green seaweed, which grows in deeper water than *Ulva*. Its dark green stems are considerably forked, and slimy to touch.

There are many freshwater green algae which are filamentous. *Draparnaldia* has clusters of branches that arise from the main filament. *Spirogyra* produces simple filaments of cells and often forms a pale green scum on the surface of ponds.

The much-branched filaments of *Cladophora* are quite common in ponds, often forming mats of vegetation. In some species, some of the lower cells are used to store food. In one related genus, the filaments are linked by means of peculiar hook cells.

One group of Mediterranean algae, *Acetabularia*, produces a large cap at the ends of its upright filaments. This cap is, in fact, a whorl of cells, above which the sporangia are produced. Like *Corallina* of the red algae, the plant is encrusted in lime.

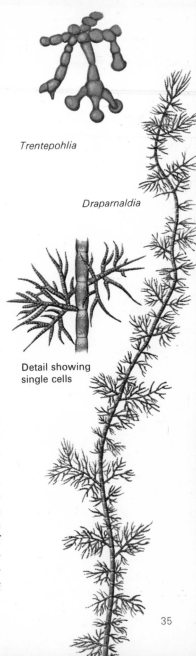

Trentepohlia

Draparnaldia

Detail showing single cells

35

The bryophytes

Mosses and liverworts are usually grouped scientifically under the heading of bryophytes. Although mosses are known to most people the liverworts mostly escape public attention as they only grow in damp shady places. With some exceptions, the bryophytes only thrive under damp conditions as they are primitive land plants and readily lose their water to a dry atmosphere.

The moss and liverwort plant, or the thallus, is the haploid generation (gametophyte). The gametes which it produces in its male and female sexual organs fuse to produce the diploid generation (sporophyte).

In the bryophytes, this remains attached to the gametophyte, and usually produces sporangia on a long stalk. When the spores are released from the sporangium, they grow into a new gametophyte, and so complete the cycle.

Life cycle of moss (A) and liverwort (B); gametophyte green, sporophyte red. 1. Moss plant and liverwort thallus 2. Production of sexual organs 3. Fusion of gametes 4. Growth of sporophyte 5. Production of haploid spores in capsules 6. Spore discharge 7. Growth of spores into new plants

Marchantia
polymorpha

Sphaerocarpos californicus, male
gametophyte *(left)* and female
gametophyte *(below)*

Riccia tricarpa

The liverworts

These are of two types, of which one is represented here by
Sphaerocarpos, Marchantia and *Riccia*. In this first type, the
thallus is a relatively simple structure anchored by hairs, or
rhizoids, which are unicellular. In contrast with the mosses,
no leaves are present, and the thallus may be spherical, as in
Sphaerocarpos, or creeping and branched. This branching may
be haphazard, or regular, and *Riccia* shows an example of a
thalloid liverwort which has regular branching. *Riccia* and its
allied genera commonly occur on the surface of ponds and
ditches, though being small they are inconspicuous. The
growth of the larger *Marchantia* results in a lobed thallus.

The sporophyte of *Sphaerocarpos* develops enclosed within
the gametophyte, and the spores are only released by decay of
the whole plant. The sporophytes of *Riccia* grow embedded
within the surface tissue of the gametophyte, but those of
Marchantia are raised on a long stalk above the thallus.

Pellia, *Riccardia* and *Fossombronia* belong to another class of liverworts, which although they are related to the leafy liverworts discussed below, appear superficially similar to the *Marchantia* type.

Pellia has four well-distributed species, and grows in a wide variety of places, usually on the banks of shady streams and ditches, though it can be found growing submerged in water. Its dark green thallus is irregularly lobed, and like *Marchantia* forms large patches wherever it grows. Its shape of growth can be considerably modified according to the particular conditions of its habitat, and it is therefore a fairly variable plant.

A mid-rib is present in the centre of the thallus, though not as pronounced as in the related *Metzgeria*. The antheridia are produced on the upper surface of the thallus, over the mid-rib and some way back from the growing points. The archegonia are positioned just behind the growing points and appear in groups that are protected by a flap.

The egg cells in the archegonia are fertilized by the sperm produced by the antheridia, giving rise to the sporophyte,

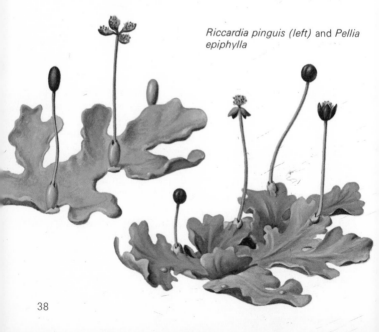

Riccardia pinguis (left) and *Pellia epiphylla*

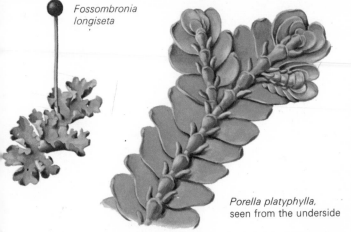

Fossombronia longiseta

Porella platyphylla, seen from the underside

which develops into a capsule. When the spores inside this capsule are mature, it is raised rapidly up above the gametophyte on a long stalk, or seta, bursting through the protective cover over the archegonia. The capsule then bursts releasing the spores, which germinate into a new thallus (gametophyte).

Riccardia is a smaller plant than *Pellia,* and some of its 280 species grow upright, with the branches differentiated into a mid-rib and wings. The antheridia and archegonia grow on special side branches. The development of the sporophyte capsule is very similar to that of *Pellia.* The thallus of *Fossombronia longiseta* is split into irregular lobes which join on to the central mid-rib; the plant therefore has something of the appearance of a leafy liverwort. In other species, these lobes are quite well defined.

In the true leafy liverworts, however, there is a definite distinction between leaf and stem, making it difficult in many cases to distinguish them from the gametophytes of mosses. Such difficulties can only be resolved by using a microscope to examine the leaves and rhizoids. The leaves of such liverworts are arranged in two overlapping rows. The antheridia and archegonia are produced in specialized shoots protected by leaves; the sporophyte capsule emerges from these when it is ready to shed its spores. *Porella* illustrates this typical structure.

The anthocerotes

This is a widespread group of about 300 species, possessing many features of both liverworts and mosses. The gametophyte is thalloid, often with crinkled edges. This thallus is usually many cells thick, comprising one type of cell, and anchored by numerous smooth rhizoids. On the lower part of the thallus there are often mucilage cavities which are filled with *Nostoc,* a blue-green alga, which gives the plant its characteristic dark green colour. The *Nostoc* cells enter the thallus through the slime pores on the lower surface.

Some anthocerotes are able to tide over unfavourable conditions by means of tubers, in which the outer cells of the thallus form a corky layer to prevent water loss.

The antheridia and archegonia are both embedded within the surface tissue of the thallus; the antheridia are enclosed within a chamber which splits open when they are ripe. The cylindrical sporophyte grows from a 'foot' embedded within the gametophyte, and its spores are produced in a central cavity. It continues to grow from its base from some time after the tip has begun shedding its spores, so that spore production is a continuous rather than a simultaneous process, and is therefore unique among the bryophytes.

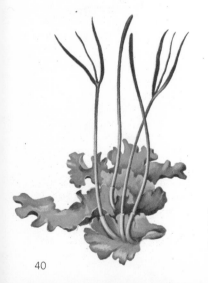

Anthoceros (left) and *(above) Notothylas orbicularis,* less than 1 cm wide, showing very young sporophytes

Sphagnum cuspidatum (above) 12 ins high. (Below) Andreaea rüpestris

The mosses

The 14,500 types of moss have several features which distinguish them from the liverworts. The spores discharged from their capsules grow into a thread-like structure known as a protonema. This produces upright leafy shoots which bear the sporophyte. The rhizoids which anchor the plant are multicellular in comparison with the unicellular rhizoids of the liverworts, and the sporophyte capsules comprise more sterile tissue which does not form spores.

Peat bogs are the result of continued growth by *Sphagnum* species over a long period; as the shoots continue to grow, the older parts die and are compressed, eventually forming peat. The several hundred species of *Sphagnum* vary considerably in their colour and size, but their general appearance is very similar, due to the fact that some of the stem leaves give rise to bunches of side branches, covered in leaves. The sexual organs arise at the apex of main shoots, and sporophytes grow on stalks of gametophyte tissue.

Andreaea is remarkable for its reddish-black coloration and its unique capsule. The small plants grow on boulders in mountainous or arctic regions under exposed conditions, and produce peculiar rhizoids to anchor their stems to the rock surface. The capsules are borne at the stem apex in common with other mosses.

Both *Sphagnum* and *Andreaea* are unusual in some of their features, and cannot be classed as typical mosses. Most of these show some degree of internal organization, which in *Polytrichum* has reached the stage of a primitive vascular system. In higher plants, the vascular system is best known in the form of wood (xylem) and bast (phloem), and is responsible for transport of substances, including food and water, round the plant as well as providing mechanical strength. For this reason, perhaps, the stems of Polytrichum tend to be longer than most mosses, and it is often found in dry exposed habitats. In contrast *Funaria, Bryum* and *Fissidens* are rather small mosses.

Bryum is commonly found in gardens and on walls, producing compact shoots which later bear capsules on stalks (setae). These capsules open by a lid which exposes a series of teeth responsible for spore dispersal. This feature of the capsule is common to practically all true mosses. The spores are, in most

Bryum capillare   *Fissidens adianthoides*

cases, all of one size, but in a few mosses (*Micromitrium*, for example) two spore sizes are produced, the smaller one developing into a male gametophyte, and the larger one into a female. This condition, which is said to be heterosporous (*hetero* means different), is of major significance in the higher plants.

The shape and colour of the moss capsules is one of the features by which they are distinguished from each other. The capsules of *Polytrichum* are elongate, and in some cases have conspicuous ridges. Many others are pear-shaped, while those of *Bartramia pomiformis* appear in the unripe stage like miniature green apples.

The variety of colour and shape in the moss plant ranges from the pale green *Mnium* to the translucent *Hookeria*; from the simple *Fissidens* to the much-branched *Thuidium*. *Thuidium*, found generally on shaded banks, changes colour in the autumn to various shades of yellow and red. Some mosses such as *Eurhynchium* form close mats, while *Leucobryum* grows in isolated hummocks. Many mosses grow on tree trunks as epiphytes attached to the bark, and a surprisingly rich variety is often found on decaying stumps and fallen trunks.

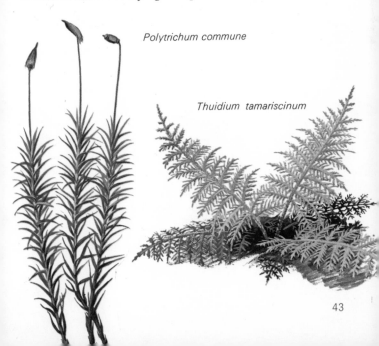

Polytrichum commune

Thuidium tamariscinum

The pteridophytes

The living pteridophytes include the ferns, horsetails, club-mosses and psilotes. There are also several classes of pteridophyte which are completely extinct, and the little that is known of them comes from examination of fossils. Although very diverse in their appearance, they share a common type of life-cycle in which the sporophyte generation is dominant, and may be represented by a fern plant, such as bracken. This is in contrast with bryophytes, where the gametophyte is the dominant phase of the life-cycle.

The life-cycle diagram here illustrates the sequence for a typical fern, but the sequence is the same for all pteridophytes. The gametophyte (in green) is a heart-shaped prothallus which produces male and female sex organs on either the same or separate prothalli. The male gamete swims in a film of water to the egg in the female organ (archegonium), and the fertilized cell develops into a young sporophyte (fern plant, in red). As this plant grows, the gametophyte dies away.

Life-cycle of ferns shown in a series of diagrams, sporophyte is red and the gametophyte is green

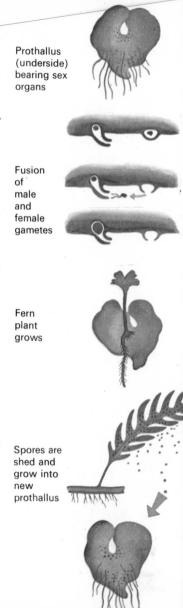

Prothallus (underside) bearing sex organs

Fusion of male and female gametes

Fern plant grows

Spores are shed and grow into new prothallus

The psilophytes

Psilophytes are known only from fossils, the first of which were discovered in 1859 in Canada. This fossil was named *Psilophyton*, a simple land plant with a creeping rhizome and aerial shoots bearing pendulous sporangia at their tips. More fossils were discovered in Scotland, and included *Rhynia, Asteroxylon,* and *Horneophyton.*

Rhynia also had an underground rhizome which bore occasional upright shoots. The shoots had no leaves or scales, and forked to give rise to cylindrical sporangia at their tips. The spores are thought to have given rise to gametophytes which possessed both male and female organs. The plants were between one and two feet high, and were presumably sporophytes as they produced spores; no gametophyte has been definitely found. One interesting fact about them is that they did not have any roots, only rhizoids similar to those found in bryophytes.

Rhynia major

Sporangium

Asteroxylon mackiei

The psilotes

These comprise two types of living pteridophyte which bear many resemblances to the psilophytes. These are *Psilotum* and *Tmesipteris*, of which *Psilotum* is found in the tropics and Australasia, and *Tmesipteris* in Australia alone. Their internal structure is almost identical, but in general appearance they can easily be distinguished.

Psilotum produces aerial shoots bearing occasional scale-leaves from a rootless rhizome. Some of the shoots are fertile, and bear lateral sporangia which appear to be fused in threes. The spores produce one type of gametophyte, which is in fact the rhizome of the plant, and bears the sexual organs. In comparison with the psilophytes, therefore, it might be assumed that the rhizomes of those plants are also the gametophytes, but no sexual organs have ever been found. *Tmesipteris*, which usually grows on trees, has pendulous leaf branches with lateral sporangia at the tips of the shoots.

As in the case of *Psilotum*, the rhizome is known to be the gametophyte as it produces male and female organs, and the young sporophyte, or prothallus, which is produced by it is

A psilote, *Psilotum nudum*
(left) and (below) *Selaginella
krausiana*, a lycopod

almost identical to that of *Anthoceros*. This fact has suggested that there may be a link between the anthocerotes and the psilotes.

The lycopods

Selaginella krausiana has delicate, much-branched shoots that produce cones of sporangia at their tips. Both large and small spores are produced (heterospory); the larger female ones are retained on the plant until after fertilization, a condition which is part of the trend towards a seed in higher plants.

Lycopodium clavatum (Club Moss) has stems that are closely covered in pointed leaves, and terminate in cones (strobili) of sporangia. The spores are all identical (homosporous). This species grows in bogs and owes its specific name to the forking of the shoots beneath the strobili. Other species grow hanging from trees.

Isoetes lacustris (Quillwort) produces leaves each year from a buried corm. The leaves are fleshy, and have a bulbous base in which the sporangia are produced. The plant is heterosporous. The first leaves of the year produce female spores, and the later ones produce male spores.

Sporangia

Lycopodium clavatum (above) and *(below) Isoetes lacustris*

47

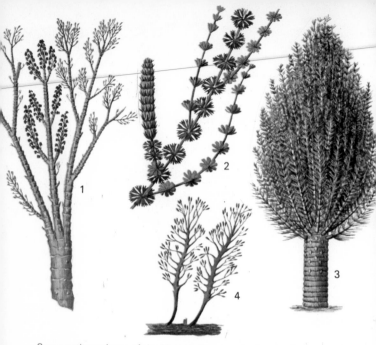

Some extinct plants of the Horsetail group. As they are known only as fossils, their colours are hypothetical. 1. Shoot of a *Calamophyton* 2. *Sphenophyllostachys* 3. *Crucicalamites* 4. *Protohyenia janovii*

The sphenopsids

Sphenopsids may be distinguished from the lycopods by the pronounced jointing of the sporophyte stems, with the leaves and sporangia produced in whorls. As in the lycopods, some species are heterosporous. Both groups therefore advanced along similar lines, and became predominant at a time when the coal measures were being formed.

Most of the sphenopsids became extinct after this time, now being found mainly in the coal seams. *Protohyenia* is often regarded as an ancestral member of this group, as the aerial shoots which arose from a creeping rhizome bore branches and sporangia in primitive whorls.

On the other hand, *Calamophyton* showed very pronounced jointing of its stem, with finely forked branches giving the appearance of leaves. The fertile branches bore whorls of sporangia in groups of up to twelve. *Sphenophyllostachys* had very prominent whorls of lobed leaves on a weak stem, some branches terminating in fertile cones of sporangia. Each whorl in this cone comprised a complex of numerous sporangia protected by bracts. *Crucicalamites* was one of a group of tree horsetails, reaching a height of 90 feet.

Equisetum is the only living type in this group, comprising about twenty-five species of worldwide distribution, though completely absent from Australasia. They are found in a wide variety of habitats, some being evergreen and others deciduous.

In contrast with other sphenopsids, the horsetails are small plants, relatively slender and with no secondary thickening. The green, ridged vegetative stems are produced from a complex underground rhizome system, and bear no recognisable leaves; these are reduced to toothed sheaths at each joint in the stem. The sheaths are not green, and the stems therefore make the food for the whole plant. The fertile shoots, which bear the sporangia in complex cones, are only green in some species and live for a shorter period than the vegetative shoots.

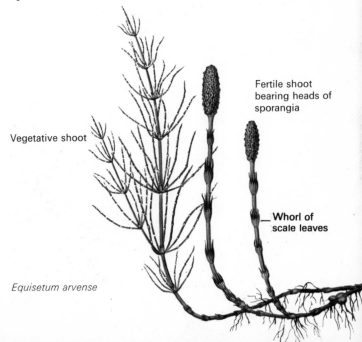

Fertile shoot bearing heads of sporangia

Vegetative shoot

Whorl of scale leaves

Equisetum arvense

Royal Fern,
*Osmunda
regalis*

The ferns (pteropsids)

Ferns, of which there are some 9,000 species are generally recognized as bearing complex fronds from an underground rhizome, with the sporangia occurring in groups on the surface of the leaf; the bracken plant *(Pteridium)* is among the best known examples. However, the variation is enormous, and many ferns would not be recognized as such if compared with *Pteridium*. The extinct fern ancestors often bore little resemblance to the typical ferns, although some of them had frond-like leaves.

Among the living ferns, *Ophioglossum,* the Adder's Tongue Fern, with forty-five species distributed over the world, produces one simple leaf each year, and gives rise

Azolla filliculoides

Marsilea

to a fertile branch terminating in a spike of sporangia. *Osmunda* forms hummocks, in which the first fronds produced each year are sterile, being followed by fertile ones, where the frond leaflets (pinnae) are much reduced and bear the sporangia. The gametophytes are comparatively large, being up to 4 centimetres, and are dark green in colour, like a thalloid liverwort.

The true ferns include *Adiantum,* the Maidenhair Fern, the filmy ferns (*Hymenophyllum* species); the tree ferns of the tropics, which may grow to 60 feet (*Cyathea* species); *Polypodium;* and *Platycerium,* the Stag's Horn Fern. This last fern owes its name to the fact that it produces two roughly circular fronds next to the tree trunk on which it grows, with projecting fertile fronds which are much branched and have the appearance of antlers. The gametophytes of the true ferns are typically heart-shaped, with the antheridia and archegonia on the lower side.

A number of unusual ferns grow exclusively in water. *Marsilea* mainly grows in shallow water, producing its four leaflets on the top of a long stalk and having the appearance of a four-leaved clover. The sporangia are enclosed in a hard, rounded structure borne at the base of the leaf.

Both *Salvinia,* the Water Hyacinth, and *Azolla* grow floating on the surface of water. *Azolla* is a minute, much-branched plant, whose overlapping leaves support colonies of a blue-green alga, *Anabaena.*

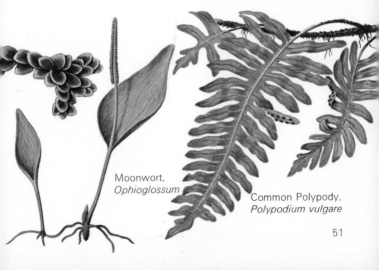

Moonwort,
Ophioglossum

Common Polypody,
Polypodium vulgare

The gymnosperms

The most familiar gymnosperms are the pines, but the group also includes the seed ferns, cycads, ginkgos and gnetales. Their unifying feature is that the heterosporous condition is taken to the point where the female gametophytes are retained on the plant until after fertilization of the egg and the formation of a seed. The female gametophyte is protected by part of the sporophyte to form an ovule. The male spores are liberated as pollen, and the male gametophyte is a much reduced structure.

The distinction between the gymnosperms and the angiosperms (flowering plants) is that the ovules are naked, and definite archegonia are still produced by the female gametophyte. About 800 types of gymnosperms are known.

The plants which are thought to form a link between the ferns and gymnosperms are the seed ferns. These extinct plants consequently shared many features of both groups; the leaves were fern-like, and cannot in many cases be distinguished from those of ferns, yet they bore true seeds. Their internal structure was, moreover, similar to the gymnosperms. Examples of this group include *Neuropteris* and *Lyginopteris*.

The seed ferns probably gave rise to two groups of gymnosperm: the cycads, many of which are living today; and a similar group which is completely extinct. This second type differed in the unique position of its cones (strobili) on the side of the trunk, and the much smaller size of its seeds.

The cycads have changed remarkably little over many millenia, and are often regarded as living fossils. The examples of *Cycas, Dioon* and *Zamia* show the general shape and structure, in which a thick stem covered by numerous leaf scars is topped by a crown of frond-like leaves, giving the appearance of a palm. In the case of *Zamia,* the trunk is very small, and one species, *Zamia pygmaea,* is the smallest cycad known. *Dioon* species vary considerably in their height, though *Dioon edule* is a fairly short plant; some species reach a height of 30 feet.

Cycas is also a variable tree-like plant, with spiny leaves that are sharp to touch. The cycad male and female reproductive organs are borne on separate plants, at the centre of the crown.

Cycas species

Dioon edule

Zamia otonis

53

Encephalartos longifolia (above) and *(below) Bowenia cerulata*

Encephalartos is a cycad restricted to Africa being an extremely slow-growing plant with some individuals calculated to be several hundred years old, yet they may only attain a height of 8 feet. The tuberous stem of *Bowenia,* buried underground, produces a number of leaves which are quite different from those of other species, as they are not like the fronds of the *Cycas* type. The reproductive cones arise apparently at the base of the leaves, just above soil level. This genus is restricted to Australia, in common with many other cycads.

In *Cycas revoluta,* the ovules are borne on modified leaves, which in *Zamia* have become a cone. The egg cells are protected by a stony layer which serves later to protect the seed.

Seeds

Female shoot

Ginkgo biloba

The ginkgos

Ginkgo is the only surviving member of a group of very ancient trees. The texture of the leaves is almost leathery, and they are lobed in a way similar to the Maidenhair Fern, from which *Ginkgo* derives its popular name (Maidenhair Tree).

The trees, which are either male or female, produce long shoots which give rise to short lateral spurs, on which the male and female structures arise. Each scale on the male cone bears two sporangia containing pollen. The female organs (ovules) receive the pollen in a special chamber, where it develops into sperm.

Fertilization of the egg cell within the female gametophyte results in the formation of a pendulous seed which falls to the ground and germinates.

The conifers

Conifers are perhaps best typified by *Pinus sylvestris,* the Scots Pine. The needle-like evergreen leaves are produced in pairs at the tips of short spur shoots. They are dark green in colour and contain resin. The occurrence of resin is a fairly general character of conifers, and in some cases is a source of turpentine. The male and female cones are produced on separate branches, the male cones liberating winged pollen, the female ones, winged seeds.

The spruces (*Picea* species) and firs (*Abies* species) are allied conifers, and include those which are used as Christmas trees. *Taxus baccata,* the Yew, is more uniformly covered in dark leaves, and usually grows as a large bush or small tree. In some of the more ancient specimens, the stems are gnarled and the centre may be rotted away. The seeds are surrounded by a bright red cup.

The tall trees of *Araucaria araucana,* the Monkey Puzzle Tree of South America, show very regular branching, where the branches are clothed in thick triangular leaves which overlap and give the tree an armoured appearance. This is a most distinctive plant, and produces its male and female cones on separate plants, like *Taxus.*

Agathis australis also has large fleshy leaves, but these are produced on the branches in two opposite rows. It is an enormous tree of up to 150 feet, producing an extremely hard wood. The Juniper, *Juniperus,* grows as a bush or small tree with sharp needle or scale leaves. The male and female flowers are on separate trees and the female plants produce blue-black

Agathis australis   Juniper, *Juniperus communis*

seeds, covered with a fine glaucous bloom, about two or three years after development of the cone.

The American genus *Taxodium,* or Swamp Cypress, is remarkable for two features: first, the production of upright growths ('knees') from the roots, which project above the surface of the water in which the plant grows; and secondly, for the strengthening of the trunk by numerous aerial (adventitious) roots which grow down and fuse on to the stem.

The redwoods, *Sequoia gigantea* and *S. sempervirens,* are the tallest trees known, and one of them is illustrated on page 5. The cypresses, *Cupressus,* have much-branched leaf shoots bearing small fleshy leaves. They are very frequently cultivated as hedges and as ornamental plants.

Yew, *Taxus baccata*

Scots Pine, *Pinus sylvestris*

Monkey Puzzle, *Araucaria araucana*

The gnetales

There are only three types of this group, *Ephedra*, *Welwitschia* and *Gnetum*. Although this group has some affinities with the angiosperms, the ovules are naked, and the gnetales are therefore included in the gymnosperms. All have separate male and female plants. *Ephedra* has about thirty species, distributed over the world, and is a wiry shrub with minute leaves.

Welwitschia is known only from a small part of South Africa, growing in extreme desert conditions. The plants, which may live for 100 years, appear malformed and apparently bearing a number of ragged leaves around a woody crown. There are, in fact, only two leaves, which become split and separated to surround the crown, and which continue to grow from their base to a length of 6 feet. The crown bears the male or female cones on stalks; no archegonia are produced. *Gnetum* is a tropical plant, growing as a creeper (liana). Its appearance is much like that of an angiosperm, though it produces strings of cones in which the female ones have no archegonia. Although it is not an angiosperm, it represents the most advanced living gymnosperm.

Welwitschia

Ephedra viridis

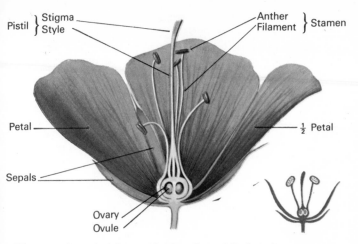

The parts of a typical flower, Meadow Cranesbill, *Geranium pratense*. In the accompanying diagram the sporophyte is shown in red, the gametophyte in green.

The angiosperms — the flowering plants

The relative dominance of gametophyte and sporophyte has been described for all the main groups of plants so far discussed. In the last group, the angiosperms (flowering plants), the alternation of generations is best understood in the light of the evolutionary trend from the algae to the gymnosperms.

In the algae, neither generation predominates, but in the bryophytes, the gametophyte is the dominant generation, and the sporophyte is a partially dependent phase which grows from it. However, in the pteridophytes, the roles are reversed; the sporophyte (fern plant) is dominant, and in some cases produces separate male and female gametophytes. The size of the gametophyte is reduced further in the gymnosperms, where it is dependent on the sporophyte, which produces separate male (pollen) and female (ovules) gametophytes. The ovules are enclosed, and bear traces of their origins; but in the angiosperms, these are enclosed by sporophyte tissue to form an ovary, and the sporophyte tissue is developed to form a structure (the flower) which will protect both pollen and ovules and secure fertilization.

The angiosperms can be divided into two main groups on

the basis of a number of features. These groups are the dicotyledons and the monocotyledons. The word 'cotyledon' applies to the leaf-like structure which is part of the seed and is responsible for nourishing the germinating embryo; monocotyledons therefore have one cotyledon, and the dicotyledons have two.

This distinction is strengthened by the fact that the leaves of the two groups are somewhat different – those of the monocotyledons are long and narrow with parallel veins and grow from the base, while those of the dicotyledons are usually broad with complex veins and grow from the tip. A comparison of the leaves of the iris (monocotyledon) and beech (dicotyledon) will demonstrate the point.

The diocotyledons

In terms of numbers of species, the dicotyledons more than equal all other plants put together. The reason for this is probably that the angiosperms are the most recently successful of the many plant groups, and fewer of them have, therefore, become extinct.

In this group, there is a tremendous variety of both herbaceous and woody plants, as shown by the buttercups and the related woody magnolias. They are among the simplest of dicotyledon flowers. The separate coloured petals and green

American Chestnut, *Castanea dentata*

Princes Plume, *Stanleya pinnata*

sepals are easily distinguished. The flowers bear a mass of stamens, and the ovary is split into units (carpels) which each contain an ovule.

In the crucifers, which derive their name from the cross-like arrangement of their usual four petals, the separate carpels are united into one ovary. Examples include the cabbages, wallflowers, horseradish and rape. The gentians are well known for the striking colour of their blue flowers. Here, the petals are united into a tube, a character common to many other families.

The umbellifers are distinguished by the way in which the minute flowers are grouped together in flat heads, borne by stalks giving the appearance of umbrella spokes. They include the caraway, carrot, hemlock, parsley and fennel.

There are many families of dicotyledons which consist entirely of trees or shrubs. The chestnuts, oak, beech, hazel and willow are a few examples, where the flowers are small in comparison with the size of the plant, and some show adaptation to wind pollination, for example hazel catkins.

Wild Fennel, *Foeniculum vulgare*

Marsh Gentian, *Gentiana pneumonanthe*

Viper's Bugloss,
Echium vulgare

Sawwort,
Serratula tinctoria

Another family which bears its flowers in heads includes the Sawwort, *Serratula*. The individual flowers within the heads are small and reduced to a tube surrounded by a calyx of hairs. The stamens and styles often project considerably beyond the head, which is enclosed in a series of scales. These scales often give considerable protection to the flowers, particularly in the case of the spiny heads of the thistles.

The poppies are among the most brightly coloured of the dicotyledons, but they are also distinctive for another feature: the sepals drop off when the flower opens. Examples include *Argemone*, *Eschscholzia* and the brilliantly blue *Meconopsis*. The complex flowers of most garden roses bear little resemblance to the wild ones, which have a simple cup of separate petals. The pear, the apple and the plum also belong to this family.

Three widespread families which have flowers in the form of

tubes are the violets, dead-nettles and figworts. Each of these families has a distinctive arrangement of petals partly related to their mechanisms of pollination. A comparison of the pansy (violet), salvia (dead-nettle) and *Linaria* or *Antirrhinum* (figworts) shows how they differ. The dead-nettles derive their name from their similar appearance to the stinging nettles.

The marrows, cucumber and loofa plant belong to the cucurbit family. In these three examples, their popular name derives from the fruit, which is very fleshy. They are all plants which climb by means of tendrils produced by the leaves. *Echium* is a member of the borages, which include the forget-me-nots. The bristled stems produce flowers which change from pink to blue as they open. Many of the borages are used medicinally. Yet another family is that of the legumes, which comprise many crop plants, such as clover, lucerne and peas. The complex flower is termed papilionate after its supposed resemblance to a butterfly. Other well-known members of this group are the gorse, broom and lupin.

(Below) Toadflax, *Linaria vulgaris* and *Argemone hispida* (right)

Tiger Lily

The monocotyledons

The lilies and their related plants form a very colourful group of monocotyledons of which the Tiger Lily is perhaps one of the best illustrations. The daffodils, tulips and similar bulbs are other examples. In all these cases, the calyx is united with the petals to form a striking perianth, which is a particular feature of this group.

The stamens of one *Colchicum* species are harvested in some regions for use in cooking as saffron, and other useful members of this family include the onion and garlic, both bulbous species. Many lilies, however, produce a rhizome rather than a bulb, including the Solomon's Seal and the Butcher's Broom. This latter plant is unusual in that it possesses

leng-like structures which are actually flattened portions of the stem. The flowers, and the red berries which follow them, are therefore situated in the middle of each leaf. The plant derives its name from the fact that the spiny tips of these modified stems are used by one species of bird to store insects it has captured.

Sedges, rushes, irises, bananas, orchids, duckweeds, bromeliads and pondweeds are other types of monocotyledons. Although so varied, they share the same basic features. Some of them, for example the orchids, are extremely specialized in their structure, mimicking the shape and coloration of insects to ensure pollination. The Flowering Rush (*Butomus*) is not a rush, but a relative of the pondweeds. The duckweeds are reduced to the form

Flowering Rush, *Butomus umbellatus*

(Below) *Calypso bulbosa* and (right) Snake's Head, *Fritillaria meleagris*

Date Palm,
Phoenix species

of a number of leaves which send down rhizoids into the water
on which they float.

Comprising over 2,500 species distributed throughout the
warmer countries, the palms are of great interest and economic
importance. Products such as dates, coconuts, and sago all
come from palms. In appearance, they are much like the
cycads, having a tall trunk topped by a crown of fronds; they
differ considerably in their structure and life history – they
are true angiosperms because their seeds are produced in fruits.
Although an ancient group, there is little trace of them in the
fossil record. However, there is a rich variety of forms.

The Traveller's Palm, *Ravenala madagascariensis,* shows
two rows of wind-tattered leaves which radiate out in a vertical
circle from the crown of the simple trunk; in contrast, the
Fan-Palm *(Hyphaene)* bears bunches of leaves at the top of a
much-branched stem.

The grasses and bamboos are another family of economically

important monocotyledons. Both types show considerable vegetative growth by means of rhizomes and stolons, a fact which is shown clearly by the way in which grasses very quickly form a lawn. The cereals include a great variety of species – oats, rye, millet, sorghum, wheat, barley and maize. Still other grasses are sources of sugar and oils.

The bamboos are used extensively as building materials. The leaves of this family range in size and shape from the minute to the enormous: they comprise a leaf blade which is attached to a stalk often tightly sheathing the stem. This gives the weak stem extra rigidity. The prairies of South America are often dominated by the Pampas Grass *(Cortaderia),* forming dense tussocks compounded of dead and living leaves which have very sharp edges. These plants often reach a height of 10 to 15 feet.

(From left to right) Festuca glauca, Sorghum, Puya

PLANT CHARACTERISTICS

The second part of this book is concerned with the different ways by which plants approach the same basic problems. These diagrams illustrate some of the problems and functions which are discussed separately in the following pages.

Strength and Protection

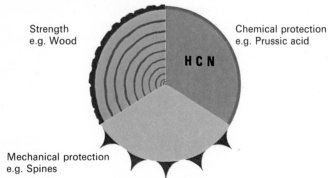

Strength
e.g. Wood

Chemical protection
e.g. Prussic acid

H C N

Mechanical protection
e.g. Spines

As plants can grow to a considerable size, they need mechanical strength to support themselves. They must also often be protected from disease and animals which eat them. Protection can involve structures such as spines, or chemicals, which deter organisms that attack them.

Drinking

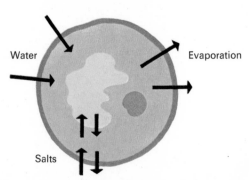

Water

Evaporation

Salts

Water is of obvious importance to plants. It is taken into the cells from the environment and lost by evaporation which may cool the plant. Salts are also necessary, and are exchanged with the environment across the cell membranes.

Feeding

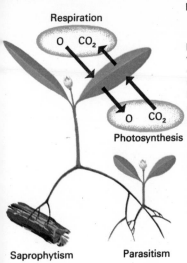

Photosynthesis is the process by which green plants make their own food from carbon dioxide, using the energy from sunlight. **Respiration** releases this energy as the plant requires it, in a process opposite to that of photosynthesis. **Saprophytism** involves the acquisition of some, or all, of the plant's food requirements from dead materials. **Parasitism** also saves the plant the need to manufacture food by photosynthesis; food material is derived from another living organism on which the parasite lives.

Breeding and dispersal

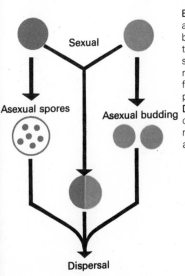

Breeding can be either sexual or asexual. Sexual reproduction is better for the plant in the long term, as it provides a greater source of variation. Asexual reproduction can involve the formation of spores, budding plantlets or off-shoots.
Dispersal is necessary to avoid overcrowding. A wide variety of mechanisms is found to accomplish this process.

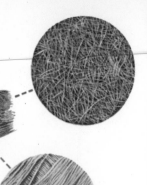

The fibres of a cell wall are of cellulose, a carbohydrate. The natural colour is off-white

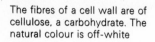

In this diagram, which illustrates the surface views of the primary *(top)* and secondary wall *(bottom)*, the fibres of the outer layer are represented in blue, the inner layer in brown. These fibres are parallel in the inner layer but in the outer layer they cross in all directions.

Strength

There is no such thing as a safe generalization in Biology; there is always at least one exception to a Golden Rule. However, it can be said that the unit of life is the cell. It is a very complex structure comprising a nucleus surrounded by a cytoplasm containing specialized structures. Throughout the cytoplasm runs a network of membranes which connect with the outermost membrane of the cell.

In plants, the cell is usually contained within a wall, whose structure reveals it to consist of numerous fibres of cellulose (true plants) or chitin (fungi), with the individual cells glued together by pectin. The effect of this wall on the cell is rather like putting an inner tube within a tyre – the tube can be inflated until it is pressing against the tyre, and, as the tyre is composed of flexible strands cemented together, the whole structure is tough, while preventing the tube from bursting.

The cell wall has, therefore, very special properties, and accordingly has two main layers, one of which comprises fibres running one way, and the other having fibres spreading in all directions round the wall. The cell is then cushioned to withstand stresses from all directions. The cell itself is inflated by water pressure, the water being drawn in by the process of osmosis as a result of the sugars in the cytoplasm. In the fully inflated state, the cell is turgid and exerts turgor pressure which can be applied as a hydraulic pressure.

In this way, plants such as Rhubarb, and certain fungi, can push their way up through concrete and asphalt with no strength other than turgor. The common mushroom grows overnight; the young young fruiting body is formed and then expanded rapidly by the uptake of water.

The importance of turgor pressure to the strength of plants can be seen in many garden plants, either when they have been transplanted or on a very hot day when the plants wilt through a loss of water. In terms of the tyre analogy, this wilting is comparable to deflating a pile of tyres which have been glued together. But just as a heap of tyres can become top-heavy, so turgor pressure alone is not

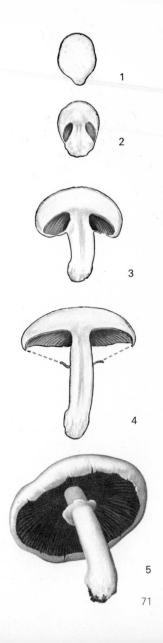

Growth of the mushroom, *Agaricus campestris.* This rapid growth is achieved by turgor pressure. 1. The button stage covered by the universal veil 2. The lamellar chambers appear 3. Veil ruptures 4. Ring or 'Annulus' 5. Mature specimen

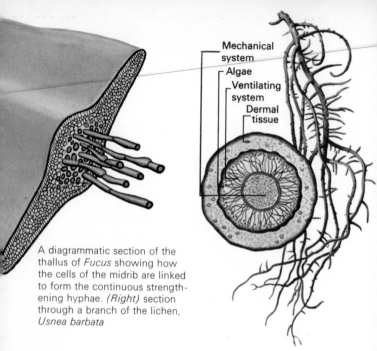

Mechanical
system
Algae
Ventilating
system
Dermal
tissue

A diagrammatic section of the thallus of *Fucus* showing how the cells of the midrib are linked to form the continuous strengthening hyphae. *(Right)* section through a branch of the lichen, *Usnea barbata*

enough to support an upright-growing plant, and therefore some cells become specialized to give added strength.

In the thalloid plants, strength is mainly a result of turgor pressure, sometimes with a number of specialized thickened cells. Many algae have thickened cells dotted throughout their thallus. *Fucus* shows this clearly. In the large *Laminarias*, which may grow to a length of 100 feet and are therefore subjected to considerable stresses from sea currents, there is a differentiated core to the thallus containing the strengthening and conducting cells. For the most part, however, the algae rely on the leathery nature of many of the thalli for their strength and protection.

The thalloid lichens show little sign of strengthening tissues, but lichens such as *Usnea*, which is tubular in its growth, have a central core of fungal cells specialized to give strength.

One group of mosses, which includes *Polytrichum*, has reached the stage of bearing leafy shoots with an internal conducting and strengthening system. The central cells have

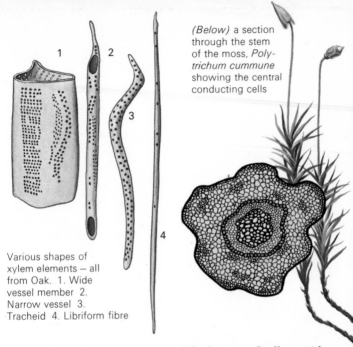

(Below) a section through the stem of the moss, *Polytrichum cummune* showing the central conducting cells

Various shapes of xylem elements – all from Oak. 1. Wide vessel member 2. Narrow vessel 3. Tracheid 4. Libriform fibre

thick walls and conduct water, while the ring of cells outside this core appears similar to the phloem of higher plants, and presumably conducts the food.

In the pteridophytes, gymnosperms and angiosperms, these systems are well differentiated into xylem and phloem. The xylem is composed of long pitted cells which are greatly thickened by deposits of the polymer lignin, and are dead. These cells (elements) are connected to each other by the pores and so form a continuous system of tubes for the passage of water and salts. The walls of lignin make the cells very strong and resilient. The structure of these elements varies from one group of plants to another.

The gymnosperms have elements known as tracheids which form the soft wood, but the angiosperms have a mixture of tracheids and vessels. The difference between tracheids and vessels lies mainly in the way the cells are joined end to end; tracheids have numerous pores in their end walls, but in vessels these walls break down to give a system of continuous tubes.

73

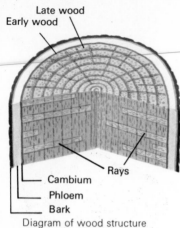

Late wood
Early wood
Rays
Cambium
Phloem
Bark

Diagram of wood structure showing the mass of xylem and its annual rings

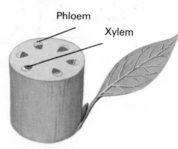

Phloem
Xylem

Diagrammatic illustration of a stem section, with the vascular bundles towards the circumference

Diagram of a root section. The strengthening vascular tissues are in the centre.

A section of a trunk shows how secondary thickening produces a vast central core of xylem with its annual rings arising from the difference in size of the elements produced in spring (large) and late summer (small). Running into the heart of the tree are numerous strands of non-woody cells (rays) which act as a passageway and a store for food. These rays connect with the bark, on the inside of which is the phloem, the food-conducting tissue.

New wood is added from the circumference of the xylem at the boundary with the phloem, where the cambium is situated. This cambium is responsible for secondary growth, both of phloem and xylem. This growth pattern produces a structure which enlarges laterally as it grows vertically from the shoot tips, and yet still retains some flexibility necessary for stability in winds.

In young shoots (no secondary thickening) the xylem and phloem are usually found together in small bundles towards the outside; but in the root, xylem and phloem alternate closely in a central core. This difference is accounted for by the different stresses roots and shoots have to bear.

Where tree branches are growing under lateral stress, such as when inclined at a steep angle, compression wood is formed. Much more wood is produced on the lower side of the branch, with the result that in cross-section the annual rings are elliptical rather than circular. Other tissues also contribute towards the strength of the stem. These include fibres and rounded cells with a heavy thickening of cellulose (collenchyma).

Collenchyma is usually found outside the vascular region, and in some cases (dead-nettles) may form distinct ridges on the outside of the stem. The extent of many vascular structures is shown in the large fruit of the loofa, where it is exposed when the flesh has rotted and the seeds dispersed; in this state, it is sold as the household loofa.

Stems and leaves also have their strengthening structures in the form of silica; in many grasses (particularly cereals), which lack secondary thickening, the stems owe much of their strength to layers of silica in the surface tissues. Specially thickened cells, sclereids, are found in a great number of plants, one example of which is the fern *Asplenium*.

Illustration *(below)* of the strengthening sclerids at the base of the leaf indentation in *Asplenium* and *(below right)* a *Luffa* skelton. When this plant is living the fibres are intermingled with the flesh of the fruit.

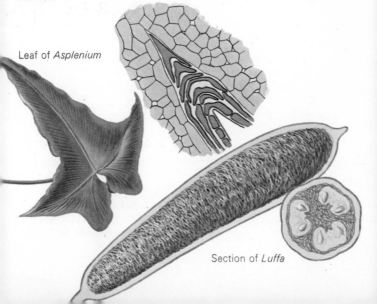

Leaf of *Asplenium*

Section of *Luffa*

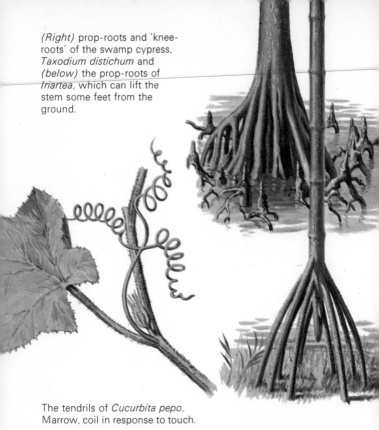

(Right) prop-roots and 'knee-roots' of the swamp cypress, *Taxodium distichum* and (below) the prop-roots of *Iriartea*, which can lift the stem some feet from the ground.

The tendrils of *Cucurbita pepo*, Marrow, coil in response to touch.

Strength in plants is therefore mainly due to turgor pressure and a woody skeleton, and enable the plant to withstand stresses; most important, it enables land plants with appreciable secondary thickening to reach considerable heights.

Many other, weaker plants are also able to grow upwards by dependence on sturdier species. In the case of the Traveller's Joy (*Clematis*), it has a weak twisting stem which smothers bushes and small trees and so reaches a height far greater than its stems could bear. The Ivy (*Hedera*) is another common example, producing small roots on its stems which allow it to climb on walls and up tree trunks. More spectacular adaptations include tendrils, which are usually specialized coiled tips

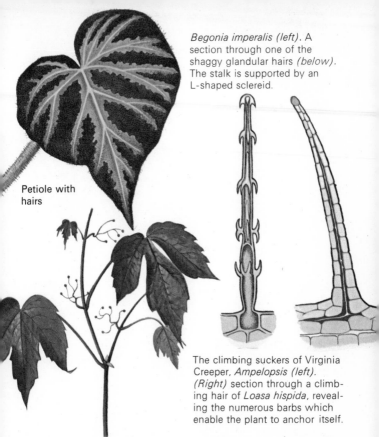

Begonia imperialis (left). A section through one of the shaggy glandular hairs *(below)*. The stalk is supported by an L-shaped sclereid.

Petiole with hairs

The climbing suckers of Virginia Creeper, *Ampelopsis (left)*. *(Right)* section through a climbing hair of *Loasa hispida*, revealing the numerous barbs which enable the plant to anchor itself.

of leaves. The tendrils of the pea plant are the commonest example, and others include the marrow, cucumber and gourds.

The related White Bryony (*Cucurbita dioica*) has unusual tendrils which first twist one way and then another. The Virginia Creeper (*Ampelopsis*) supports itself by means of sucker-pads. Exactly how these pads function is something of a mystery. The Rattan Palms are unusual in that they produce leaves, which have whips that anchor the leaves to nearby trees and literally drag the stems up with them. The spines produced on many stems (for example, Blackberry) help to anchor otherwise smooth stems which would slip from their supports; the same feature is present in *Loasa hispida*.

The protection of *Ulmus carpinifolia* is bark, of *Zombia antillarum*, spines.

Protection

Plants have evolved a variety of defences against their natural enemies – predators, parasites, pests and extreme environmental conditions. These defences include devices to trap harmful insects, poisons to kill attackers or to render the plants obnoxious, rapid wound healing, insulating layers, spines, barbs and stinging glands.

One structure which fulfils a number of these demands is the bark of trees. This layer is composed of dead, corky cells which form a barrier preventing water loss and invasion by many parasites.

A considerable number of trees and shrubs have spines, thorns, or barbs to protect them from penetration and being eaten. Perhaps one of the most spectacular examples of this is the palm *Zombia*, whose leaf bases rot and leave spinous fibres which project at various angles. *Berberis* and *Euphorbia* also have sharp, woody spines which act as a defence mechanism.

The thistles are well covered in spines, particularly around the flower heads. The protection this affords them is clearly seen in pasture, where they usually grow untouched. The stinging glands of *Urtica dioica* (Stinging Nettle) are tipped by a brittle cap which snaps off when touched, and causes the injection of stinging acid.

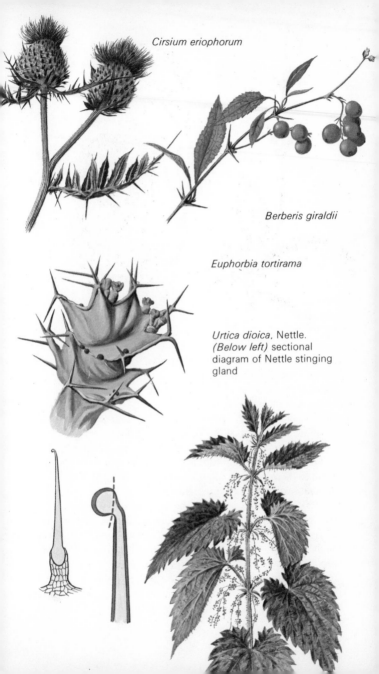

Cirsium eriophorum

Berberis giraldii

Euphorbia tortirama

Urtica dioica, Nettle.
(Below left) sectional
diagram of Nettle stinging
gland

Silene nutans

Hydnophytum montanum (Siam)

The protection of flowers from animals that in some way affect their functioning is an important factor in ensuring successful reproduction. The nectar produced by flowers to entice pollinating insects is often raided by other insects which play no part in pollination. To prevent this, many plants have sticky stems, as in *Silene nutans,* which trap any small animal climbing up the stems to the flowers.

This trapping of insects must not be confused with that of plants which actually digest such prey for their nourishment, or harbour bacteria which do the job for them (carnivorous plants). A number of plants have fused leaf bases, forming a cup at each joint or node in the stem. These cups collect water, which forms a barrier to the advance of climbing insects such as ants; this is clearly illustrated in the Teasel, where the cups are often full of drowned insects. The surface of many plants is covered in a mass of hairs which also help to prevent the passage of small animals; the flowers themselves may be similarly covered, ensuring that only flying pollinators

(Above) Acacia sphaerocephala showing the presence of ants in the spines. *(Below)* a stem portion, with ripe fruits, of *Opuntia jamaicensis*

reach the pollen and nectar.

The protection of fruits is obviously important to the success of any plant, although in some cases the fruits need to be eaten in order to stimulate their germination. Succulent fruits are obviously the most susceptible to being eaten, and a variety of structures serves to protect them. The coconut illustrates how the embryo and its supply of food can be protected by a hard shell. Similarly the fleshy fruit of the *Opuntia* cactus is covered in bristles which become embedded in the flesh of any animal foolish enough to eat or touch it.

A surprising number of plants harbour colonies of ants which serve as a living defence mechanism in return for food or shelter. Several examples will be discussed later, but two are relevant here. The first concerns *Hydnophytum,* a tropical plant which houses ant colonies in its swollen stem bases. These insects aggressively defend their home, and in so doing protect the plant. A similar situation occurs in many tropical palms and in one *Acacia,* ants live in the hollow stem spines. Any animal which disturbs the tree causes the ants to rush out to the attack.

Besides structural methods of defence, there are many chemicals which protect plants due to their toxic or obnoxious effects. The fact that so many poisons and drugs come from plants is evidence enough of the vast number of dangerous chemicals which they manufacture. Hemlock, strychnine, hallucinogenic drugs and curare are a few of the most famous examples. In many cases, their possible protective role is pure speculation; but it is difficult to see how plants would have evolved unnecessary chemicals against the efficient pressure of natural selection – by inference, they must have some use.

One recent example of how modern research is clarifying this problem is that of the 'juvenile hormone' produced by a particular conifer. This hormone prevents caterpillars which eat the foliage from maturing, and hence reproducing. This 'Peter Pan' mechanism, therefore, is a most effective defence against pests. The poisonous chemicals in some plants are lethal to any species of animal, as in *Amanita phalloides*, the Death Cap Mushroom. But the poisons of many plants are dangerous to some animals and not to others.

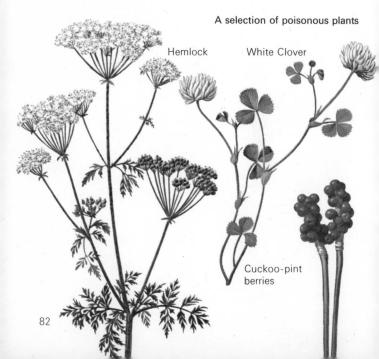

A selection of poisonous plants

Hemlock

White Clover

Cuckoo-pint berries

This apparent drawback can, in fact, be an advantage, as it may pave the way for a special relationship between the plant and one or two particular species of animal. Thus, the Cuckoo-pint, *Arum maculatum*, produces bright red berries poisonous to most animals save the thrush. This bird is therefore the distributor of the seeds. It is surprising how many plants are dangerous to livestock, or affect their yield. Bracken is poisonous to grazing animals, and is thought to contain a cancer factor.

The horsetails are similarly poisonous to livestock, while Yew causes many fatalities among cattle. The drugs from Deadly Nightshade and the Foxglove which are used in medicine can be fatal if too large a quantity is taken. Many plants release small quantities of prussic acid when damaged; some strains of the White Clover are able to produce this poison and so are resistant to slugs, which attack only the non-toxic varieties. Apple seeds (pips) also produce this chemical, but a considerable quantity would have to be eaten to produce any noticeable effect. Resistance to disease and pests also varies as much within species as between species.

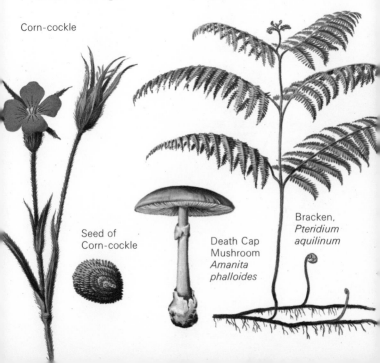

Corn-cockle

Seed of
Corn-cockle

Death Cap
Mushroom
*Amanita
phalloides*

Bracken,
*Pteridium
aquilinum*

In Duckweed, *Lemna*, the chloroplasts move in response to light intensity.

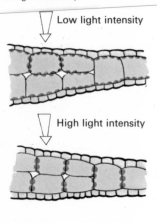

Low light intensity

High light intensity

Sun's light

Feeding

Most plants are able to manufacture their own food by the process of photosynthesis. The energy of light is harnessed by pigments, most commonly chlorophyll, to provide chemical energy for the incorporation of simple molecules into complex compounds such as starch.

In true plants, this energy is used to 'fix' carbon dioxide (0·03% of the atmosphere) involving a simultaneous release of oxygen from water. Therefore, provided with an adequate supply of water, carbon dioxide and mineral salts, plants are independent of other organisms for their food.

In higher plants, photosynthesis occurs mainly in the leaves, which are adapted to a high intake of light and carbon

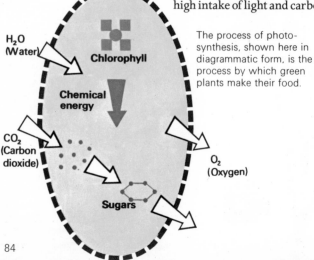

H_2O
(Water)

Chlorophyll

Chemical energy

CO_2
(Carbon dioxide)

Sugars

O_2
(Oxygen)

The process of photosynthesis, shown here in diagrammatic form, is the process by which green plants make their food.

Toothwort, *Lathraea squamaria*, is parasitic on Hazel roots and *(below) Euphrasia officinalis* is a parasite of grass.

dioxide. One such example is that of the fern *Hymenophyllum*, where the complex structure of the leaf presents a large surface area to the atmosphere. The chlorophyll is located in chloroplasts within the cells, which in *Lemna* change positions according to the light intensity, as very strong light can be harmful to the pigments.

There are numerous examples where a plant's ability to manufacture its own food has been partially or totally lost. Such plants are saprophytic or parasitic. Those which draw food directly from other living organisms are said to be parasitic, and are attached by special structures to their host plant.

Certain plants of the fig-wort family have the appear-

(Right) Hymenophyllum malingii, a piece of a leaf and a section through a pinna

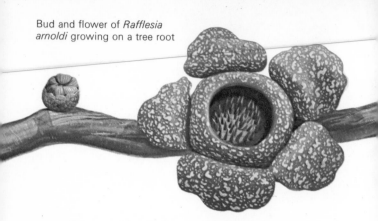

Bud and flower of *Rafflesia arnoldi* growing on a tree root

ance of a normal green plant, but they are attached by special roots to other plants which supplement their food supply. *Euphrasia*, the Eyebright, *Rhinanthus*, the Yellow Rattle and Red Bartsia are members of this group of partial parasites.

Both *Lathraea*, the Toothwort, and *Rafflesia* are examples of total parasites. *Lathraea* is a parasite of the Hazel, to which it is attached underground, and only appears in the spring when it produces its flowers. The leaves are peculiar hollow structures, whose function, since they cannot make any food, is obscure. The giant *Rafflesia* is visible only as a foetid flower up to a yard in diameter. It grows on the exposed roots of some tropical trees, nourishing itself within the root and eventually producing a bud which expands rapidly.

The same considerations apply to the bacteria – the parasitic ones are responsible for most diseases. Once they secure entry to the plant or animal tissues, they multiply rapidly, using food derived from dead cells, blood or sap. Some bacteria can double their numbers once every half-hour. The toxins which many produce as a result of their activity may kill surrounding tissues, or create a breakdown of regulatory systems in the case of animals, leading to fevers. The effect of the disease may be temporary, lethal or permanent, and the bacterium may infect specialized tissue or the whole body.

The diptheria bacterium grows in the throat, but sends toxins to the rest of the body; the tuberculosis germ is usually restricted to the chest, but may spread elsewhere. Bacterial diseases of plants include the soft-rots and wilts of vegetables, and the galls seen on many plants result from growth hormones produced by the invading bacteria.

In the lower organisms, invasion of the host enables the parasite to take in its food requirements directly from the blood or sap, and also in many cases to break down the host's structure partially or totally by secreting digestive enzymes. The toxins produced by many parasites kill the host tissue in advance of the organism, ensuring little resistance and a ready food supply. Parasites which can only live in contact with the host are said to be obligate, while those which can live also saprophytically on dead material are said to be faculatative. Some fungal parasites extract their food from the host by means of special invading suckers (haustoria). *Armillaria* is an obligate parasite of many trees, including the apple. Its rapid growth within the roots, and later the stem, soon leads to the death of the tree and production of the basidiocarps.

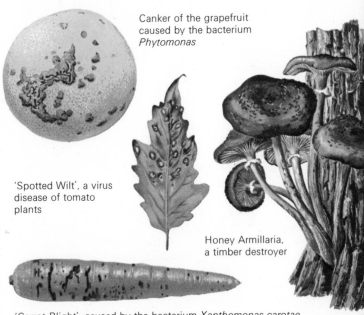

Canker of the grapefruit caused by the bacterium *Phytomonas*

'Spotted Wilt', a virus disease of tomato plants

Honey Armillaria, a timber destroyer

'Carrot Blight', caused by the bacterium *Xanthomonas carotae*

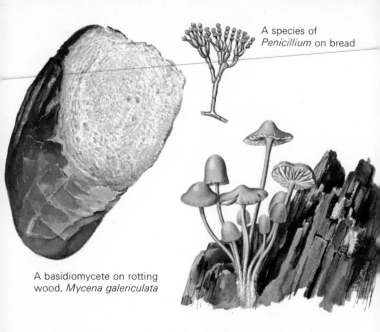

A species of *Penicillium* on bread

A basidiomycete on rotting wood, *Mycena galericulata*

The saprophytes often follow in the wake of the parasites, utilizing the host remains, or feeding on products such as dead leaves, dung, leather or food. The intestines of all animals contain a 'flora' of micro-organisms which feed on ingested food, and apparently import some degree of resistance to disease. In many cases, this flora is essential to the digestion process of the animals which harbour them (for example, the ruminants).

In the tropics, due to the high humidity and temperatures, fungi readily attack clothing, breaking it down into simple substances for absorption. The secretion of enzymes for this process can easily be demonstrated by culturing certain fungi or bacteria on starch, and staining to show how the starch round their colonies disappears.

Cellulose is one of the commonest waste materials, and numerous organisms are able to digest it for their own use. The soil is, therefore, the commonest source of saprophytes, as most of the waste cellulose occurs as leaves and straw which are buried by earthworms, or form a surface litter.

Many basidiomycetes are found as saprophytes on tree

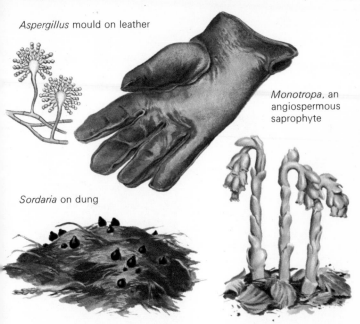

Aspergillus mould on leather

Monotropa, an angiospermous saprophyte

Sordaria on dung

stumps, including *Fomes, Polyporus* and *Pleurotus*. The bracket, or shelf, fungi digest the cellulose and lignin of wood by secretions from their mycelium, and extrude their basidiocarps usually as perennial brackets on the bark, adding new portions each season. The storage products within the wood are a useful source of food.

The Yellow Bird's Nest, *Monotropa*, is a dicotyledonous saprophyte associated with the mycorrhiza of the beech, pines or willows. The plant is yellow, consisting of a simple stem covered in slightly overlapping scales, at the top of which are produced the pale yellow flowers. This plant obtains all its nutrients from the soil and the fungus without photosynthesis.

In contrast with the photosynthesis of higher plants, (involving the use of energy from light to fix carbon dioxide into more complex compounds, with water broken down into oxygen) the photosynthetic bacteria are able to replace either carbon dioxide or water by other simple molecules, without the release of oxygen. Some of the purple sulphur bacteria use hydrogen sulphide in place of water to fix carbon dioxide.

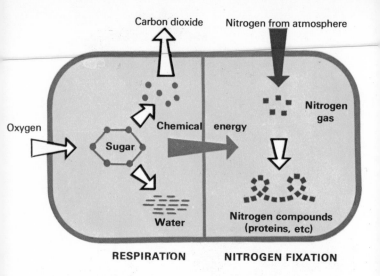

This process takes place in two parts, and in the first, sulphur is released and stored either inside or outside the cell for use in the second part if the supply of hydrogen sulphide stops.

Similarly, carbon dioxide may be replaced by other simple carbon compounds such as acetic acid, which is the case in some other purple bacteria. A few pigmented bacteria are able to utilize hydrogen gas in place of water, fixing either carbon dioxide or other carbon compounds. Many of these bacteria will only live in the complete absence of oxygen – air is lethal to them.

The energy stored in complex compounds by photosynthesis can be subsequently released by the process known as respiration. Respiration is a feature of all organisms, as all require energy, and in the higher forms involves oxygen as the final oxidizing agent. Respiration is therefore effectively the reverse of photosynthesis; carbon dioxide and water are released from the complete oxidation of sugars.

Among the bacteria, to which oxygen is often lethal, respiration is modified to function anaerobically, so that

Sulphur bacteria utilize hydrogen sulphide (H_2S) as an energy source. Yellow grains of sulphur can be seen in the cells.

The light given off by some species of toadstool is sufficient to produce a photographic image like the one above.

compounds are not completely oxidized to carbon dioxide and water. Yeasts, too, can respire anaerobically, producing alcohol and carbon dioxide from sugars.

The acetic acid bacteria produce acetic acid from sugars, while other groups produce butyric acid, citric acid or oxalic acid. Among the inorganic compounds used by them to provide energy are sulphates, nitrates and sulphur. Some of this energy may be released as light, as in the case of luminescent bacteria and fungi, and therefore the cycle of light-photosynthesis - sugars - respiration - light is completed.

The fixation of nitrogen is another important process, as nitrogen is an element essential to all organisms. Certain bacteria are able to convert nitrogen gas into useful solid compounds, and therefore play an important part in the nitrogen cycle. The sources of nitrogen available to other organisms are therefore products ultimately derived from minerals, and nitrate produced by the effect of lightning on atmospheric nitrogen. This fixation requires considerable energy, which is derived from the oxidation of sugars.

Many plants have sticky stems, flowers or leaves which trap small animals, particularly insects. Relatively few of these, however, actually digest them and absorb their remains; such plants which digest trapped animals are termed carnivorous, of which there are about 450 species. Some fungi are carnivorous, catching their prey by a loop, but most of these plants are angiosperms. The mechanisms which effect the trapping and digestion are quite varied, but they can loosely be divided into two types, the passive and the active.

In the passive type, the prey is simply caught by a sticky secretion, or falls into a trap; no movement of any part of the plant is involved. In the case of *Byblis,* insects are caught by a viscid secretion produced by stalked glands on the stems, leaves and even flowers. Other glands secrete juices which dissolve the captured animals and absorb them. The pitchers of *Nepenthes* are modified leaves, and collect water into which small animals and insects fall and drown prior to their digestion. The peculiar 'lobster-pot' traps of *Genlisea* are produced in shallow water, hanging down rather like tuberous, hollow roots, with an opening at the tip. As the prey passes down the trap, it is digested and absorbed by the plant. The rosette leaves of *Pinguicula,* the Butterwort, like *Byblis* bear numerous sticky glands. However, some degree of active response to the trapped prey is shown in the form of the edges of the leaves partially inrolling. Digestive enzymes are believed to be secreted by the glands. A similar system is found in the sundews, *Drosera* species, in which tentacles are produced over the surface of the leaf and are tipped by glands. Other glands are produced both on the surfaces of these tentacles and over the leaves. The tentacles respond to the presence of food by curling over and trapping it until digestion has taken place.

Two other interesting active mechanisms are encountered in the Venus Fly Trap, *Dionaea,* and the Bladderwort, *Utricularia*. The leaves of *Dionaea* are hinged, bearing at their margins a number of tentacles. When an insect alights, the leaf rapidly closes, rather like a butterfly shutting its wings, enabling digestion to take place.

1. Venus Fly Trap, *Dionaea muscipula* 2. Pitcher plant, *Nepenthes alba marginata* 3. *Pinguicula* 4. *Sarracenia* 5. *Byblis gigantea*

Mosses beneath trees rely for minerals on those leached by rain from the tree leaves.

Besides the major requirements of carbon dioxide or other organic compounds, water, nitrogen compounds, light and usually oxygen, plant nutrition involves a wide range of minerals. Calcium is an essential part of cell walls, while silica is also deposited here. Magnesium is an integral part of chlorophyll, while iron, potassium, zinc, copper and maganese are some of the elements involved in the functioning of enzymes. Plants deficient in any of these elements display deficiency symptoms which may be characteristic.

A shortage of magnesium results in a low level of chlorophyll, and the plant is said to be chlorotic. A deficiency of zinc will lead to peculiar flower formation in Clover. And, of course, shortages of potassium (potash) or phosphates give symptoms dreaded by every gardener.

However, excess can be as harmful as shortage, or even lethal. The spoil heaps of metal mines contain extremely high concentrations of minerals, and hardly anything will grow on them, as these minerals penetrate the plant and inhibit its functioning, or prevent the uptake of other elements. Yet, strains of some

Chlorosis is a mineral deficiency causing yellowing of the leaves.

Agrostis tenius (above) illustrating the ability of some plants to adjust to the minerals on a mine slag-heap.

plants can be found that have derived a mechanism which enables them either to tolerate high levels of metals within them, or to exclude them from the plant.

Most minerals enter the plant by the roots. In lower plants, these are represented by rhizoids, but in higher plants the roots bear numerous minute hairs at their tips, presenting a large surface area to the soil. Mineral salts in solution are taken into the roots, and carried via the xylem throughout the plant. The pattern of uptake is often specific for a particular plant, though plants do not only absorb elements which they require. The mechanisms of uptake are still somewhat obscure and controversial. *Sphagnum* cell walls behave like an ion-exchange resin, such as those used to soften hard water, and exchange hydrogen ions for salts. The surrounding water thus becomes acid. Carnivorous and parasitic plants obviously obtain their mineral requirements from their prey or host, while mosses growing on dry soil beneath trees often depend on the drops of rain which drip from the leaves above.

Drinking

The fact that many plants comprise over 90% water indicates the importance of this compound to plant life; in fact, to all living organisms. As a fluid, with hydraulic properties, it is responsible for turgor pressure, an important element in plant strength. As a liquid with a neutral pH (neither acid or alkaline), it is the ideal solvent for many chemical reactions. It is a requirement of photosynthesis, and a product of respiration. Under acid conditions, it behaves as a weak alkali, and under alkaline conditions it behaves as a weak acid; its freezing and boiling temperatures are suited to the range of temperatures most commonly found on this planet, so that water evaporates from the soil to the sky, and condenses as rain to come back again to the soil, rivers and seas.

The importance of water is therefore obvious, but one problem remains – availability. Plants cannot move in search of water. At the most, they can extend their roots to new

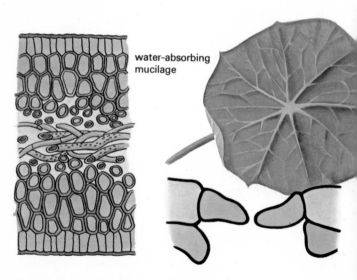

water-absorbing mucilage

Part of a section through the thallus *(left)* of the brown seaweed *Fucus. (Right)* transverse section of one of the numerous hydathodes in the leaf of *Tropaeolum majus*, Nasturtium

sources. If they grow in a region where water is not always plentiful, they have to conserve it, and a variety of mechanisms has evolved to achieve this.

As far as water availability is concerned, plants which grow immersed in water, or float on its surface, enjoy the best conditions; but this does not allow for the possibility of the habitat occasionally drying up, or, in the case of green plants, the problem of the availability of light and carbon dioxide.

The cells of water plants are very thin, and water is freely exchanged; their surfaces often contain special pores, water stomata, which aid this process. Aquatic fungi, bacteria, algae and bryophytes need no special structures, as their cells are freely permeable to water.

Aquatics which become exposed at certain periods – seaweeds for example – often contain mucilage cells which are thought to act as water stores. Their surfaces are also covered in mucilage to restrict evaporation. Many higher plants take in more water than they can lose by evaporation and nutrition, and possess water pores, or hydathodes, on their leaves.

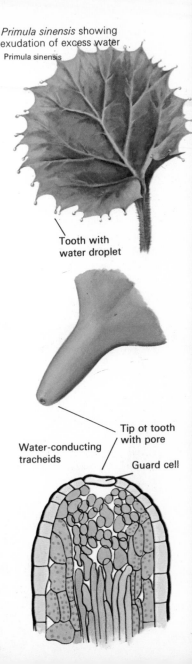

Primula sinensis showing exudation of excess water

Primula sinensis

Tooth with water droplet

Tip ot tooth with pore

Water-conducting tracheids

Guard cell

Excess water is exuded as droplets, a process termed guttation, and much of the dew seen on some plants is a result of it. Salts are sometimes excreted with this water from hydathodes, encrusting the leaves and stems. The whitened leaves of some Saxifrages are due to calcium salts deposited in this way.

The lower land plants do not have proper water-conducting systems, and rely upon capillary attraction between cells. The rhizoids function as the first link in this chain of conduction, and take up water rapidly. *Sphagnum* has no rhizoids in the mature plant, and relies on conduction by external cells. Some species possess specialized empty stem cells with numerous pores; in some cases these cells are termed retort cells for obvious reasons. Water is therefore rapidly drawn from cell to cell up the stem. In other species, dead cells in the leaves form the conducting system, and absorb water up to a weight twenty times that of the plant itself.

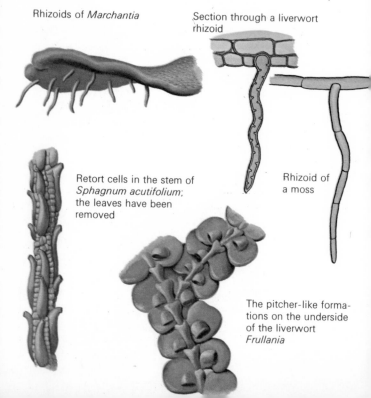

Rhizoids of *Marchantia*

Section through a liverwort rhizoid

Retort cells in the stem of *Sphagnum acutifolium*; the leaves have been removed

Rhizoid of a moss

The pitcher-like formations on the underside of the liverwort *Frullania*

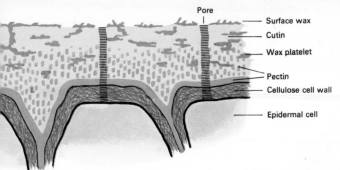

Pore

Surface wax

Cutin

Wax platelet

Pectin

Cellulose cell wall

Epidermal cell

The structure of the cuticle and its relation to the epidermal cells *(above)*. *(Right)* the surface wax on many plants often takes the form of rodlets at right-angles to the surface. This illustration is magnified by about 10,000.

The leafy liverworts, have their pairs of overlapping leaves arranged either above or below the following pair, so that conduction can be facilitated up or down the stem according to the way in which the plant grows. *Frullania* has a small pitcher at the base of each leaf, which is thought to function as a water-store.

The exposed surfaces of all land plants are covered by a protective coat known as the cuticle. It is an elastic skin punctuated only by the breathing pores, or stomata. Basically, it is a sponge of cutin whose pores are filled with wax.

In cross-section, the cuticle can be seen to be attached to the outermost cell walls by a layer of pectin, with which it is inter-woven. Even the cells within leaves are coated with a thin cuticle. Although it swells in water, the cutin forms a framework for a water-repelling structure which plays an important part in water retention.

The internal wax deposits are often extended as a surface 'bloom' (such as that seen on grapes and plums) which can be quite complex. The surface wax of the sugar cane, for example, is present as a layer of rodlets. It is the wax which is really responsible for water retention, and if removed allows con-

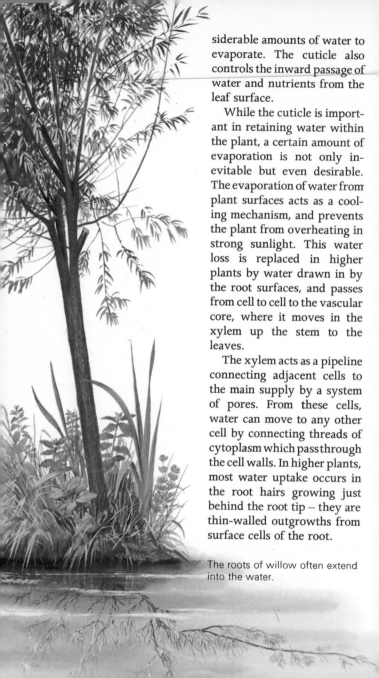

siderable amounts of water to evaporate. The cuticle also controls the inward passage of water and nutrients from the leaf surface.

While the cuticle is important in retaining water within the plant, a certain amount of evaporation is not only inevitable but even desirable. The evaporation of water from plant surfaces acts as a cooling mechanism, and prevents the plant from overheating in strong sunlight. This water loss is replaced in higher plants by water drawn in by the root surfaces, and passes from cell to cell to the vascular core, where it moves in the xylem up the stem to the leaves.

The xylem acts as a pipeline connecting adjacent cells to the main supply by a system of pores. From these cells, water can move to any other cell by connecting threads of cytoplasm which pass through the cell walls. In higher plants, most water uptake occurs in the root hairs growing just behind the root tip – they are thin-walled outgrowths from surface cells of the root.

The roots of willow often extend into the water.

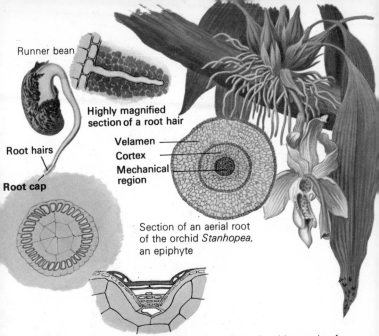

Runner bean

Highly magnified section of a root hair

Root hairs

Root cap

Velamen
Cortex
Mechanical region

Section of an aerial root of the orchid *Stanhopea*, an epiphyte

(Above) magnified view at leaf surface of a water-absorbing scale of *Vriesia psitticina* a bromeliad. *(Right)* section of scale.

The water roots produced by some trees near water perform the same function. Those of the willows are often bright pink, and absorb water in considerable quantities. The rooting systems of many desert plants extend for considerable distances in search of water. Rooting systems are very adaptable and grow towards a water supply – buried wood holds large amounts of moisture, and is usually honeycombed with roots.

A great many tropical orchids grow on the trunks and branches of trees, where much of their water supply comes from the humidity present under the tree canopies. They therefore have special aerial roots which absorb the atmospheric moisture by means of a thin-walled tissue several cells deep, the velamen. *Vriesea* is unusual in having its leaf surfaces covered in absorptive scales. When dry, each scale forms a cup, so that water falling on it is retained. The scales rapidly absorb the water, and in so doing change shape to form a convex cap which helps to reduce water loss.

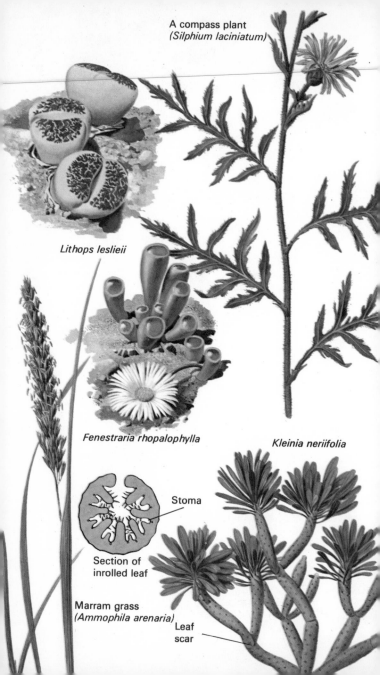

A compass plant
(*Silphium laciniatum*)

Lithops leslieii

Fenestraria rhopalophylla

Kleinia neriifolia

Stoma

Section of
inrolled leaf

Marram grass
(*Ammophila arenaria*)

Leaf
scar

The shortage of water in arid climates has a marked effect on the lives of the plants growing there. In many areas water is available only at one season, often torrentially. Consequently, this short season is a period of intense activity for the plant life, both for growing and for storing water.

Some desert and scrub plants behave as annuals – growing, flowering, and setting seed within the space of the wet season. Others exist as bulbs, and produce leaves and flowers only when water is plentiful. Many shrubs and cacti spend the dry season as naked stems which sprout leaves under favourable conditions. *Kleinia neriifolia* is an example where the leaves are deciduous, dropping off in drought, and new ones appear after rain. Others include the Crown of Thorns, *Euphorbia splendens,* and many other euphorbias.

The true cacti have no leaves, only spines, and store considerable quantities of water. Few stomata are present in the thick cuticle, as little carbon dioxide is taken in. The compass plants present an unusual example of a growth pattern which protects the plant from excessive sunlight. Each nearly-vertical leaf is twisted on its side, exposing only a small area to the sun. Their name is derived from the fact that the plants often point their leaves in a North-South direction. Examples include *Silphium* and the Prickly Lettuce. Many Australian plants adopt this protective habit.

In some cases, desert plants are so well adapted to their environment that they cannot be distinguished from their natural background. The stone plants such as *Lithops leslieii* have the same shape and colouring as many pebbles, and normally are passed unnoticed.

Some of the most familiar examples are species of *Conophytum* and *Fenestraria*. The succulent leaves are completely fused in pairs, enclosing the stem and developing leaves, and giving the appearance of a leafless stem. The top of the plant is often speckled, and may contain a translucent structure, or window, which admits some light to the rest of the plant. During the dry season, the plant appears to die, as the outer pair of leaves go brown, but as soon as water is available these split open to reveal a fresh pair of leaves. Other means of protection include sunken stomata in a very thick cuticle, or the ability of the leaves to roll up in dry conditions *(Ammophila)*.

Breathing

The life processes of plants involve respiration and photosynthesis, for which there must be an exchange of gases between the plant and its environment. For photosynthesis, carbon dioxide must be taken in and oxygen released; and for respiration the flow of these gases is reversed. In addition, many organisms, such as some bacteria, require hydrogen sulphide or hydrogen. Ethylene is also released by many tissues. There is, therefore, a considerable traffic of gases between the cells and their environment. The balance of exchange between different gases varies not only between different plants, but in any one plant throughout the day.

In sunlight, the rate of photosynthesis is much greater than that of respiration, making a net influx of carbon dioxide and loss of oxygen; but at night, respiration is not accompanied by photosynthesis, and the exchange involves a nett loss of carbon dioxide. In lower and simpler plants, gases are simply exchanged through the cell or plant surface, and no special structures are therefore required. With increase in size and complexity, diffusion

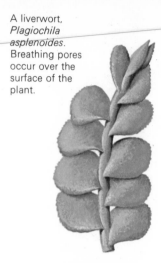

A liverwort, *Plagiochila asplenoides*. Breathing pores occur over the surface of the plant.

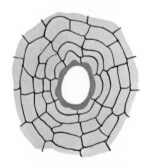

Fegatella conica, surface view of an air pore *(above)* and vertical section *(below)*

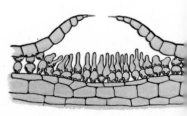

through the outermost cell walls is not sufficient to supply all the plants requirements – in a tissue of tightly-packed cells, the inner ones would suffer both from a lack of certain gases and an excess of others by continued production.

Such tissues therefore incorporate numerous small spaces which connect with each other and with the outside, often by pores. In lower land plants, these pores are simple holes, but in higher plants these pores have become specialized stomata.

The trend of plant evolution has been from water to the land: the problems of water availability, as we have seen, are therefore mostly associated with higher plants which have colonized land. The need to exchange gases with the environment for the life processes consequently accelerates the loss of water – if carbon dioxide and oxygen can diffuse freely in and out of the plant, so can water. How, then, can the land plants compromise on this problem? The answer lies in the cuticle. As a water-repelling structure which allows the diffusion of carbon dioxide, the cuticle with its stomata allows unimpeded flow of carbon dioxide, while retaining some control over water loss.

The lower land plants have simple pores, often character-

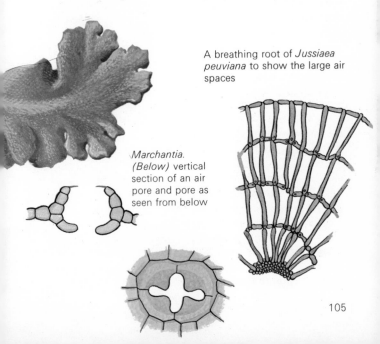

A breathing root of *Jussiaea peuviana* to show the large air spaces

Marchantia. *(Below)* vertical section of an air pore and pore as seen from below

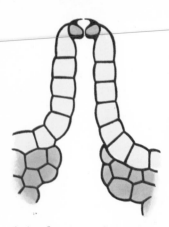

Raised stoma on *Cucurbita pepo* (left) and (right) Sea Lyme Grass, *Elymus arenarius*, showing air chamber of stoma over-arched with two green mesophyll cells.

istic of a given plant. Those of *Marchantia* are barrel-shaped comprizing sixteen to forty cells which form a lip above and below the outside layer of cells. The lower lip projects into an air chamber, separated from others in the thallus.

On the floor of each chamber are scattered the photosynthetic cells. In surface view each pore appears cross-shaped because of the bottom row of four projecting cells. In contrast, the stomata of *Fegatella conica* are raised on a stalk-like projection.

The stomata of plants higher than the bryophytes are pores formed by only two cells, termed guard cells. The variable thickening on the guard cell walls allows them to vary their shape according to their turgor. Because of this their behaviour is the opposite of what would be expected – in the turgid state the pore is fully open, while a loss of water closes it. Thus the wilted plant closes its stomata and prevents further water loss.

The guard cells are usually the only green cells in the outermost layer of the plant (epidermis) – exactly how this effects their behaviour is not known, but carbon dioxide concentration plays a part. The stomata are therefore able to change their size according to different conditions. Partial closing affects the rate of carbon dioxide and oxygen diffusion very little, while significantly cutting down water loss. The higher plants have therefore found a fairly efficient compromise between gas exchange and undesirable water loss.

Stomata are found mainly on leaves, but also occur on green stems and even occasionally on roots. Below the stomata are cavities which lead through air spaces to all the cells of the leaf. Gases can therefore diffuse from any cell and find their way out through the stomata, via these air spaces.

The stomata of conifers, as shown by the example of a species of juniper, are quite distinctive while sharing the same basic features as those of angiosperms. Both grasses and conifers have stomata arranged in rows along the leaf. These are connected in a regular fashion by air passages formed by arched cells. The cavities below the stomata are also roofed in by arched cells (as in *Elymus arenarius,* the Sea Lyme Grass) which are thought to strengthen the stomatal tissues.

In a number of plants which grow in damp shady places, or have leaves which are easily wetted, the stomata are raised on stalks. *Cucurbita pepo* illustrates how the positioning of stomata in this way helps to increase the loss of water and exchange of

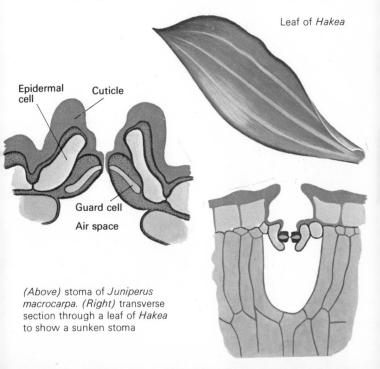

Leaf of *Hakea*

Epidermal cell

Cuticle

Guard cell

Air space

(Above) stoma of *Juniperus macrocarpa. (Right)* transverse section through a leaf of *Hakea* to show a sunken stoma

gases, while possibly preventing the pores from becoming blocked by drops of water.

The bark of many twigs is pitted by small breathing pores or lenticels. In the twigs of the Ash the lenticels are easily visible as lighter spots against the grey stem. *Sambucus,* the Ground Elder, has very conspicuous lenticels which appear as light-coloured warts on the stem. Each wart is a loose mass of cells that break the uniform covering of tightly packed cork cells.

The spaces between these cells presumably allow air to move through the bark to the living tissues underneath. In actively growing twigs this is probably essential, as air can only reach the stem cells by this route – air taken in by the leaves has too far to travel to allow sufficient exchange. Each lenticel thus serves a particular portion of the stem. In the Beech, they are complex, with alternate layers of cork and non-cork cells.

Elder, *Sambucus nigra*, showing the lenticels as small warts in the bark

(Below) section of an Elder lenticel to demonstrate the loosely-packed cork cells which allow the stem to breathe

A mangrove swamp with closely-packed pneumatophores growing from the roots, through the airless mud

Plants growing in water can only obtain their oxygen and carbon dioxide from the gases dissolved in the water, and both these gases are present in lower concentrations than they are in the air. Although this is sufficient for many plants, a number of ways have evolved for avoiding this problem. One way is obviously to produce some leaves floating on the water surface or projecting in the air, like the Water Lilies and Arrowhead. Another is to have air storage tissues as a part of the underwater structure. The stems and leaves of a number of aquatics contain this spongy honeycombed tissue, which also adds to the buoyancy of the plant. Mangrove roots project pneumatophores above the water-level for breathing. These spongy tubes are filled with connecting air spaces which open by a pore to the atmosphere.

Transport and Excretion

The movements of gases in and out of the cell are accompanied by the movements of liquids and the solids dissolved in them. The need for a complex transport system obviously does not arise in unicellular organisms, as food moves about the cells by a combination of diffusion and transport across the membranes.

Waste products, toxins and digestive enzymes are transported across the outer cell membrane, or by connecting pores from cell to cell to the outside of the plant. Even useful food can be secreted in this way – the unicellular alga *Chlorella* has been shown to secrete amino acids (the building bricks of protein) to the surrounding water. Nectar is also secreted by cells from structures known as nectaries, which are usually part of the flower. Nectar is a sugar solution whose concentration varies from 25 to 75 per cent. Flower nectaries may be exposed, as in *Ruta graveolens,* or concealed to protect the nectar from thieving insects.

Higher animals have a blood-circulatory system which allows food and oxygen to be pumped round the body by a heart. It comprises two types of pipeline – arteries and veins – which form a continuous system. By contrast, the transport system in plants is much more simple: water for transpiration and photosynthesis is drawn up mainly in the xylem from the roots, while food passes from the active leaves to the stem, roots and embryo leaves via the phloem. The two systems are not directly connected, and function quite separately, but a certain amount of leakage between them does occur. The

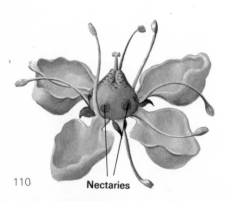

Nectaries of *Ruta graveolens* seen as discs at the base of the ovary

Nectaries

active cells in the phloem are the sieve tubes and their companion cells.

The sieve tubes are strands of cells joined together by modified end walls – sieve plates – containing numerous pores. Each sieve cell is controlled by its own companion cell, as transport in the phloem is an active process. Food is believed to pass both up and down each sieve tube so that movement through the plant is flexible, both for short distances to

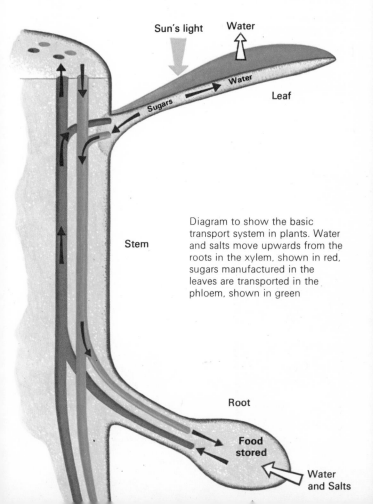

Diagram to show the basic transport system in plants. Water and salts move upwards from the roots in the xylem, shown in red, sugars manufactured in the leaves are transported in the phloem, shown in green

adjoining cells or from the leaves to storage tissues in the stem or the root.

Some of the larger algae possess a tissue similar in appearance to the phloem of higher plants, and its function has been assumed to be the same. Most bryophytes do not have a conducting tissue.

The food transported in the phloem is almost exclusively sugar – sucrose. Other systems occur in plants for the transport or storage of specialized products. Thus, the resin canals typical of pines transport resins and gums, including turpentine. A cross-section of a pine needle shows the canals into which the resins are secreted.

A number of angiosperms have systems for transporting latex; the individual cells of the system are often much branched, and easily recognizable. The rubber-producing trees and the spurges ooze latex if wounded – the latex of the common Garden Spurge can be seen by breaking the stem, when the milky liquid flows from the wound. The tapping of rubber trees by slits in the trunk releases latex which can be collected for making rubber. Apart from its properties of closing wounds in contact with the air, it is not known what importance latex has for the plant, but it has been suggested that it acts as a food reserve.

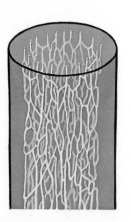

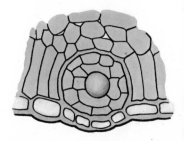

Laticifers in *Euphorbia* contain a milky latex and form a honey-combed system throughout the plant *(left)*. *(Below)* transverse section of *Dictamus albus* showing glandular activity

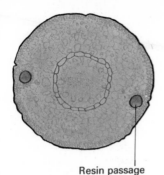

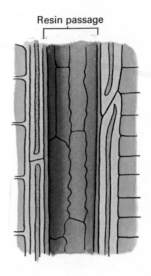

Resin passage

Resin passage

Resin passages in a leaf of a pine. In some pines these passages contain a source of turpentine

Special substances are also secreted or excreted into individual cells. Calcium oxalate, calcium carbonate, tannins, oils and mucilage are products commonly found in such cells. They are often present as crystals or bodies suspended from the cell wall. The peculiar spherical bodies found in some leaf cells of *Dictamnus albus* are an example of structures secreted into internal cavities or glands. In this way, leaves accumulate considerable quantities of apparently useless substances during their life, and many are shed with the leaf. It has often been claimed that this is one way in which higher plants excrete waste products. Nobody really knows whether such substances are waste, or whether they are storage products. Under these circumstances it is difficult to say whether they are excreted or secreted, as the term secretion is applied to useful substances and excretion to waste products. However, the wall materials released by the plant in order to coat its cells are certainly secreted, as they are useful. These substances include cellulose, lignin, pectin, silica, cutin and waxes, and in some cases have been shown to be transported from the cells via tiny vesicles, or sacs.

Breeding

Viruses do nothing but breed by invading host cells – between each cycle of breeding they display no other properties of living organisms, and can hardly be said to be living. Yet when a virus invades a suitable cell to breed, it breaks down the cell's organization and uses it to manufacture more of itself.

Reproduction in viruses is a two-step process; each virus comprises nucleic acid and a shell of protein, and these are manufactured separately before assembling them to make complete virus units. Once this is accomplished, the host cell ruptures, and the new viruses are released. This is the lytic cycle, and thus embraces a very primitive kind of feeding and breeding. Thus, some two hundred viruses may be produced.

Under some conditions, however, virulent types will not multiply, but attach themselves to the nucleic acid of the host,

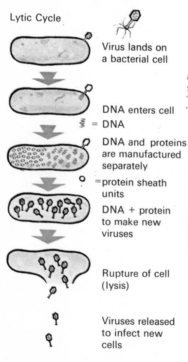

Lytic Cycle

Virus lands on a bacterial cell

DNA enters cell

🐾 = DNA

DNA and proteins are manufactured separately

o =protein sheath units

DNA + protein to make new viruses

Rupture of cell (lysis)

Viruses released to infect new cells

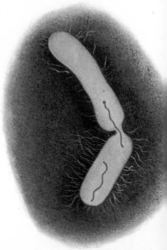

Escherichia coli, a bacterium, showing the passage of the 'male' chromosome into the 'female' cell

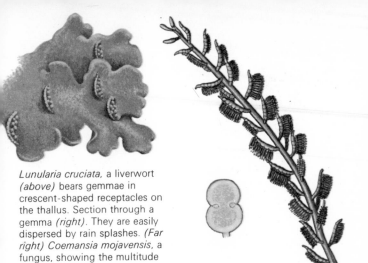

Lunularia cruciata, a liverwort *(above)* bears gemmae in crescent-shaped receptacles on the thallus. Section through a gemma *(right)*. They are easily dispersed by rain splashes. *(Far right) Coemansia mojavensis*, a fungus, showing the multitude of asexual spores

and remain there in harmony with the host until some change in the environment stimulates it to multiply and kill the host cell. This process is best seen in the bacteria, where the bacteriophage may become part of the looped chromosome.

As sexual reproduction in the bacteria involves the transfer of a 'male' chromosome to a 'female' cell, this vegetative virus can be transmitted too, although the entire male chromosome is rarely completely transferred. This partial transfer is an unusual feature, as other organisms generally involve the fusion of equal male and female gametes. A particle thought to be related to viruses is also often part of the bacterial chromosome, and its presence makes the chromosome a 'male'. This particle, the fertility factor, can also carry the drug-resistance factors which make the bacteria resistant to various drugs – the resistance for up to eight drugs may be carried here. The interbreeding between various bacterial species enables the resistance to spread from group to group, and is a serious hazard to the fight against disease.

Breeding is normally thought of as a sexual process, but vegetative reproduction is very important, including the production of rhizomes, budding or spore formation. In the lower organisms spores allow considerable spread of fungi and

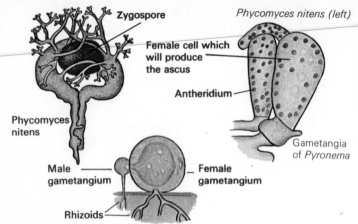

Zygospore

Phycomyces nitens (left)

Female cell which
will produce
the ascus

Antheridium

Phycomyces
nitens

Gametangia
of *Pyronema*

Male
gametangium

Female
gametangium

Rhizoids

Rhizophidium couchii

bacteria, but sexual reproduction is a shuffling of the pack of genes, and therefore an important part in the process of variation from which nature makes its selection.

It is hardly surprising that a group as diverse as the fungi has an equally diverse variety of breeding mechanisms. The situation is further complicated by the fact that some fungi produce the sexes on separate mycelia, while others are hermaphrodite. Sexual fusion may also involve distinctive separate gametes, or simply nuclei from some of the hyphae.

Among the lower fungi the most primitive condition is found in examples such as *Olpidium,* a parasite of vetches. The gametes are identical in appearance and move by means of flagella. The product from fusion, the zygote, germinates to infect the host once more. In *Allomyces,* an aquatic fungus related to *Saprolegnia,* the two motile gametes differ in size. Which is male and which is female? Unfortunately we judge everything by our own standards. To overcome this problem we can refer to mating strains rather than male and female sexes. The hyphae of opposite mating strains of some Mucor-type fungi, *Phycomyces* for example, come together and fuse to produce a zygospore which has a thick-walled resistant coat. Only opposite strains can mate. In the case of *Rhizophidium couchii* one type of gamete is larger and contained in an enlarged hyphal tip, while the other gametes are simply nuclei contained within smaller hyphae.

The smaller hyphae grow towards the larger ones and fuse with them. In some cases the smaller hyphae are known as antheridia (male) and the larger ones containing the egg cells as oogonia (female). The male vegetative hyphae of *Achlya* are stimulated to produce antheridia by a hormone produced in the female cells; the antheridia then secrete a hormone in response which causes the oogonia to be formed – in this way, altogether four different hormones are involved before sexual fusion occurs, as additional hormones are also required in attracting the antheridia to the oogonia and then in the delimitation of both the male and female organs.

The ascomycetes and basidiomycetes bring together a number of different nuclei by fusion of hyphae. These nuclei do not fuse immediately and growth continues until sexual hyphae arise and fusion takes place. The sexual cells of *Pyronema* show this in ascomycetes. From the hyphae in which nuclear fusion has occurred, arise the asci or basidia.

In asci the zygote nucleus divides to give commonly eight spores, while the nucleus in each basidium generally extrudes four spores at the tip of the cell.

As most algae live in water, they do not have to guard against many of the problems facing land plants, and, like the acquatic fungi, are therefore able to produce simple gametes. Within each main group, with the exception of the red algae, a series of both motile and non-motile gametes is found – some motile

Sequence *(from left to right)* to show the development of the basidium and basidiospores. The initial stages involve the fusion of two nuclei.

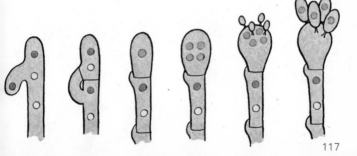

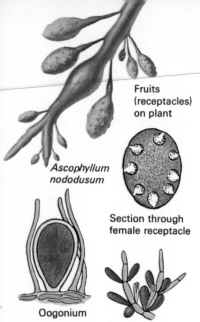

Fruits (receptacles) on plant

Ascophyllum nododusum

Section through female receptacle

Oogonium

Group of antheridia. These occupy a receptacle on a "male" plant

Ascophyllum nodosum is dioecious; sexes on separate plants

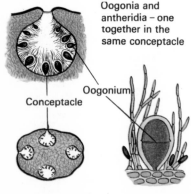

Oogonia and antheridia – one together in the same conceptacle

Oogonium

Conceptacle

Section through a receptacle

gametes being identical *(Chlamydomonas, Cladophora* and *Ulva)* and others differing in size *(Codium)*. The filamentous *Spirogyra* fuses its cells in a general manner similar to that of many fungi; one cell empties its contents into another, and the resulting fusion produces a zygote. *Chara,* the Stonewort, produces its gametes in specialized structures known as antheridia (male) and oogonia (female). The same situation exists in the brown algae *Ascophyllum, Pelvetia* and *Fucus*. In these cases the antheridia and archegonia develop in internal pits opening to the surface by pores.

At low tide the drying of the plant causes contraction of the pits, which squeezes out the antheridia and archegonia. Fusion therefore takes place outside the plant. The red algae have the most highly

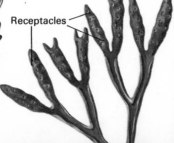

The fruiting head of part of the plant, *Pelvetia*, a monoecious seaweed

Receptacles

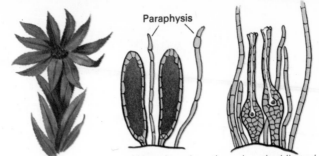

Mnium hornum

(Above) sections through antheridia and archegonia *(right)* of *Mnium,* a moss

developed reproductive structures. The antheridia release non-motile bodies which drift in the water currents and may become attached to a special projection from the oogonia. They are also unusual in that fertilization occurs inside the plants.

In one form or another the gametes of the land plants are produced in antheridia and archegonia. The archegonia are really modified oogonia in which only one egg is usually formed and retained until after fertilization. In bryophytes they are flask-shaped, with a long narrow neck surrounding a tube leading down to the egg at the bottom of the flask. The antheridia consist of a head borne on a stalk – in the head the motile gametes (sperm) are produced. The positioning of these organs varies throughout the group, but usually they are borne on the outer surface of the plant rather than wholly or partially embedded as in the higher plants. As usual, there are some exceptions to the rule in *Riccia, Pellia* and *Anthoceros.*

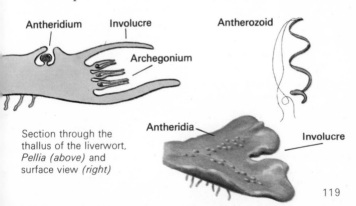

Section through the thallus of the liverwort, *Pellia (above)* and surface view *(right)*

119

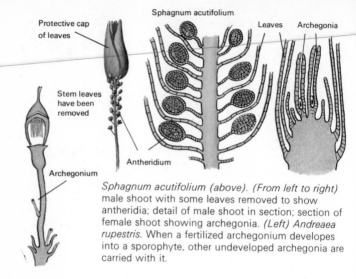

Protective cap of leaves

Sphagnum acutifolium

Stem leaves have been removed

Leaves   Archegonia

Archegonium

Antheridium

Sphagnum acutifolium (above). (From left to right) male shoot with some leaves removed to show antheridia; detail of male shoot in section; section of female shoot showing archegonia. *(Left) Andreaea rupestris.* When a fertilized archegonium develops into a sporophyte, other undeveloped archegonia are carried with it.

Marchantia and some of its allies are unusual in producing their sexual organs on special stalks, while *Sphaerocarpos* forms its organs within pear-shaped bracts. The sexual organs of *Andreaea* develop in the usual way of mosses, but after fertilization the developing embryo (sporophyte) is raised on a stalk which carries some of the other archegonia with it. In order to achieve fertilization the male gamete must first swim to a ripe archegonium – for this it needs a film of water and is attracted by chemicals. The antheridia and archegonia of *Sphagnum* are borne on separate branches, either on the same or different plants. Each antheridium is protected by a leaf and has a long stalk, while the archegonia are protected by a cup of large leaves. The male gametes are liberated by rupture of the top of the antheridium.

By way of contrast, the sexual organs of the anthocerotes are protected by being sunken into the gametophyte tissue behind the growing point, the male organs being completely enclosed in small chambers. At maturity the roof of this chamber breaks down, exposing the antheridia which in turn split to release the gametes. Each archegonial pore is surrounded by a funnel of mucilage, whose function is not known.

In the ferns, the sexual organs are borne on the prothallus,

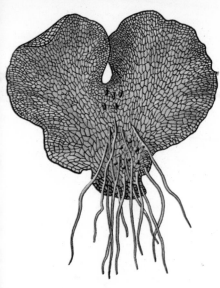

Underside of the prothallus of a fern. The archegonia are situated near the cleft, the antheridia among the rhizoids. Size less than 1 cm

Open archegonium of fern with ripe egg

the heart-shaped gametophyte. They are typically found on the lower surface, with the archegonia around the cleft and the antheridia scattered towards the apex. The male gametes have numerous flagella in contrast with the two flagella of the bryophytes, and are released by the tip, or cap cell, being pushed off. The possession of a motile gamete, therefore, means that the ferns are still dependent on a film of water to allow the male gamete to swim to the egg. As the sexual organs are situated on the lower side of the prothallus, this film of water will usually be present, but in the few cases of those fern allies where the antheri-

Antheridium filled with immature sperm

Single sperm with its many cilia (flagella)

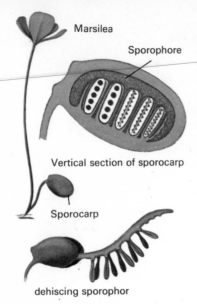

Marsilea

Sporophore

Vertical section of sporocarp

Sporocarp

dehiscing sporophor

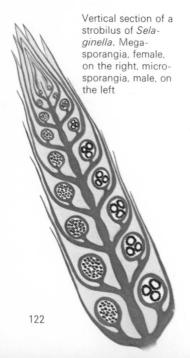

Vertical section of a strobilus of *Selaginella*. Megasporangia, female, on the right, microsporangia, male, on the left

dia and archegonia are borne on separate prothalli, the problem is greater. The fusion of the egg cell and sperm results in a zygote which grows out of the archegonium to become the fern plant.

The sporangia produced on the leaves of the fern plant contain the spores which will grow into new prothalli. In true ferns all these spores are identical and will grow into bisexual prothalli. But many pteridophytes produce two types of spore, the smaller forms a male gametophyte and the larger a female one. This is the case in *Selaginella*, where the two spore types are produced separately in different sporangia. Furthermore, both types of spore do not grow into a large structure such as a prothallus, but the gametophyte develops within the spore, and there produces its sexual organs.

In some instances the female spore is not released from the plant until one of its archegonia has been fertilized. The bean-shaped structures produced by the leaves of *Marsilea*, a fern ally, also contain two types of sporangia. Both eventually release their spores, which grow like *Selaginella* to produce minute gametophytes within them.

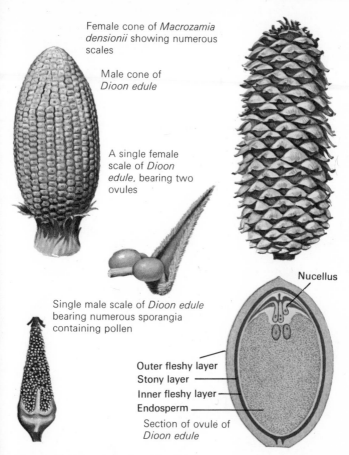

Female cone of *Macrozamia densionii* showing numerous scales

Male cone of *Dioon edule*

A single female scale of *Dioon edule*, bearing two ovules

Single male scale of *Dioon edule* bearing numerous sporangia containing pollen

Nucellus

Outer fleshy layer
Stony layer
Inner fleshy layer
Endosperm

Section of ovule of *Dioon edule*

The gametes produced by the male gametophyte then fertilize the eggs retained within the female spores.

A similar condition exists in the related *Salvinia*, the Water Hyacinth. In this way the sexes are separated on to different gametophytes, together with a reduction of the gametophyte generation. However, little reduction has occurred among the pteridophytes in the size of the sexual organs themselves.

A further stage in plant evolution can be seen in the gymnosperms. Following from the reduction of the gametophyte in some ferns, those of the gymnosperms are even smaller,

Spruce, *Picea excelsis*

A *Pinus* pollen grain highly magnified

Yew, *Taxus baccata*

Female shoot

Male shoot

Pollen

Detail of seed

Douglas Fir, *Pseudotsuga taxifolia*

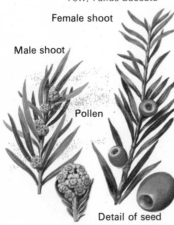

though archegonia are still recognizable. The sporangia are organized into distinctive male and female cones, while the female spores are retained on the plant in naked ovules until a seed has been produced.

The male spores are the pollen, which is usually carried to the female cones by wind. Pollen is trapped in the sticky chamber at the top of each ovule, and there germinates as a gametophyte. Often, motile gametes are produced from these spores, but in some cases reduction has proceeded far enough to do away with sperm, and there is simply a fusion of nuclei.

The most significant difference between the gymnosperms and lower plants is that male spores, rather than vulnerable sperm, are transferred to the female cones. In the pines, the Yew (*Taxus baccata*) shows the tremendous number of pollen grains which are released from the male cones to be blown to the

Female cone

female ones. Some male cones release literally millions of spores.

The small group including *Ephedra, Gnetum* and *Welwitschia* is advanced, in some cases having no archegonia at all; there is very little trace of the gametophyte left. This reduction simplifies the sexual process, making it less susceptible to the environment.

The structure of the angiosperm flower has already been described: how, then is this structure important in breeding? Most angiosperms are insect pollinated – either pollen or nectar attracts the insects from flower to flower. The colours of the petals also play an important part, although the colours we see are not necessarily those seen by other animals. Bees and birds are sensitive to different colours: this fact is illustrated by the presence of the red *Delphinium* in America, where the flowers are pollinated by humming birds, and of exclusively blue strains in Britain, where bees are the pollinators.

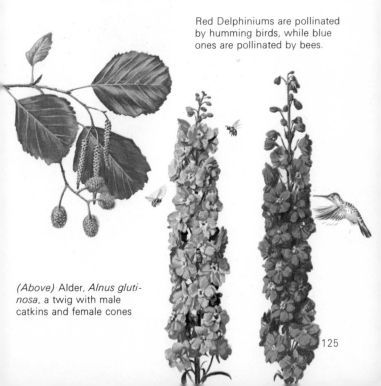

Red Delphiniums are pollinated by humming birds, while blue ones are pollinated by bees.

(Above) Alder, *Alnus glutinosa*, a twig with male catkins and female cones

125

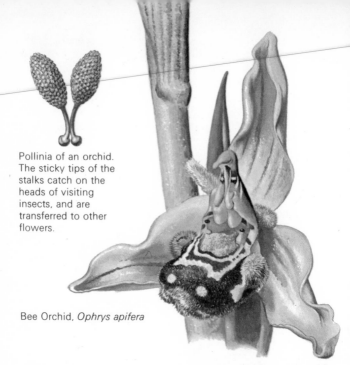

Pollinia of an orchid. The sticky tips of the stalks catch on the heads of visiting insects, and are transferred to other flowers.

Bee Orchid, *Ophrys apifera*

The absence of petals or sepals is common in the wind-pollinated trees, which often produce catkins suitable for the wind dispersal of pollen. When the pollen alights on the top of the ovary, on the styles, it germinates to produce a pollen tube which grows down towards the ovules. Fusion of nuclei takes place sooner or later to give both an embryo and a food reserve. No sperm or archegonia are produced at any stage, and reduction of the gametophyte has reached its climax. The variations in angiosperm breeding are slanted towards different methods of pollination and seed production.

Nectar and pollen are the usual bait offered to pollinators, but even foetid smells are found attractive by some insects. The Cuckoo Pint not only attracts some insects by a foul stench but traps them to ensure pollination. They slip down inside the flower and are unable to climb out until the flower wilts, when they become dusted with pollen for transfer to other flowers. The bright colours of flowers attract pollinators and guide them to the pollen or nectar, and often prevent the inside of the flowers from being too dark, for many insects avoid darkness. The complex flower of *Ceropegia* illustrates the presence of 'windows' to achieve this. Some violets are able to produce normal sexual flowers in one season and non-sexual flowers in another; the latter are small and colourless and never open to set seed.

Pollination can take place within the same plant (self-pollination) or between different plants (cross-pollination). The prevention of self-pollination can be achieved by segregating the sexes in different flowers or plants, or by allowing the anthers and styles to mature at different times. The sexes of some *Begonia* species are segregated among the flowers on the same plant, the male flowers growing above the female ones. In the event of cross-pollination failing, pollen from the male flowers above can ensure successful setting of seed.

Although wind is a common pollinating agent, the role of water is relatively insignificant. The most frequently quoted example of water pollination is that of *Vallisneria,* an aquatic angiosperm. Minute male flowers are released underwater and float to the surface where their stamens are exposed to the female flower.

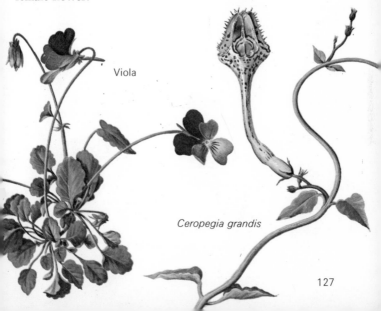

Viola

Ceropegia grandis

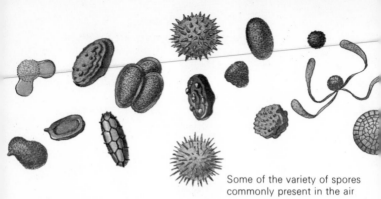

Some of the variety of spores commonly present in the air

Dispersal

To prevent excessive overcrowding and competition between individuals of the same species, seeds or spores from the parent plant must be dispersed. Often this involves only a very short distance. There is also the need to breed with other populations to ensure hybrid vigour. For any organism which cannot move these needs are achieved by an active method of dispersal, such as explosive mechanisms, or by passive dependence on animals or agencies such as wind and water.

Wind is one of the most important dispersal factors for plants and their allies, as can be seen by trapping a sample of air-borne spores; there are countless millions in the air we breathe, as sufferers from hay-fever can testify. Any person

Dispersal of *Cyathus*. A raindrop falls into the cups of the fungus, the ripe spore mass is then splashed out and its trailing tail catches on a grass stem.

Cylindrospermum stagnale, a filamentous blue-green alga, produces a large, resistant spore, or heterocyst.

who has tried to grow sterile cultures in a laboratory also knows how difficult this can be, due to the spores of fungi and bacteria present in the atmosphere. The chains of asexual spores produced by fungi are easily distributed by air currents. Rain splash is another factor which plays an important part in passive dispersal. In this way, for example, the spore masses of the fungus *Cyathus* are catapulted to another site.

Viruses may be spread from one host to another by pests such as rats or aphids, and quite commonly by breath or contact. Usually many dispersal agencies are involved. For example, foot and mouth disease is spread in a variety of ways, but which is the most important is still uncertain.

Many viruses are still dangerous after considerable periods of burial or exposure, and bacteria can also tide over unfavourable periods by forming special spores called endospores. Endospores are formed within the cells and their walls are heavily coated with calcium. In such a state they can survive high temperatures, complete dryness and harmful radiation, and therefore survive the vagaries of dispersal.

The blue-green algae produce endospores or distinctive special cells which germinate to produce a new plant. Many

Dark-staining endospores developing within cells of bacilli

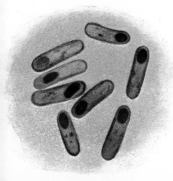
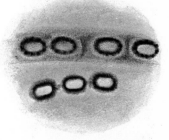

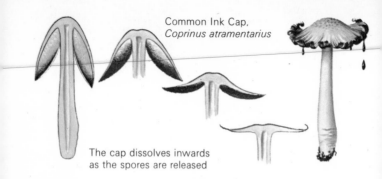

Common Ink Cap,
Coprinus atramentarius

The cap dissolves inwards
as the spores are released

algae are capable of forming resistant dispersal structures, such as zygotes or individual modified cells from the thallus.

A common method of active dispersal in fungi is that of water-squirting. In most ascomycetes this takes the form of ejecting the sexual spores from the asci by turgor pressure; as the top of the ascus dissolves or bursts the spores are forced out by the sudden release of liquid under pressure. The asci of *Sordaria* are enclosed in a 'flask', and expand one at a time, pushing to the neck of the flask where the spores are dispersed to a distance of about 20 centimetres. In common with many fungi, the fruiting bodies of *Sordaria* bend towards the light to ensure that the spores are discharged at a suitable angle.

Among the lower fungi there are few examples of water-squirting only involving asexual spores. One example is

Sordaria, a fungus *(left)* in which the asci explosively discharge their spores in turn. The spores of *Entomophthora coronata (right)* are discharged by turgor pressure.

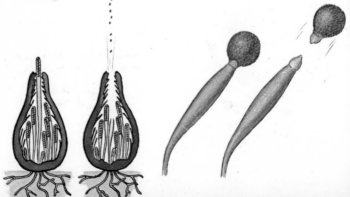

Pilobolus, where the sporangium is produced at the tip of a bulbous hypha. This hypha bursts at the tip, shooting the sporangium for a considerable distance.

Another mechanism is that involving sudden changes in the shape of the hypha bearing the spores. The spore of *Entomophthora coronata* is ejected by a suddenly bulging outwards at the point where the spores joins the hypha. Tension between tissues can act as a catapult, as in the basidiomycete *Sphaerobolus.* The fruiting body splits open to reveal the spore mass in a cup composed of six layers. Tension between these layers finally results in the spore mass being ejected to a distance of up to 18 feet due to the inside of the cup turning completely inside out. But the commonest discharge mechanism in basidiomycetes is that way in which a tiny drop of water is secreted below each basidiospore before it is thrust away. Basidiospores of the Wheat Rust, *Puccinia graminis,* discharged in this way will infect the Barberry, producing submerged flasks

Diagrammatic section of *Sphaerobolus stellatus* before dispersal *(top). (Above)* the complex structure releases its spore mass violently as it dries out.

(Right) section of *Puccinia graminis* in barberry illustrating droplet of sugar and spores.

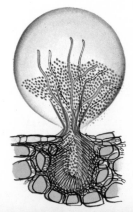

131

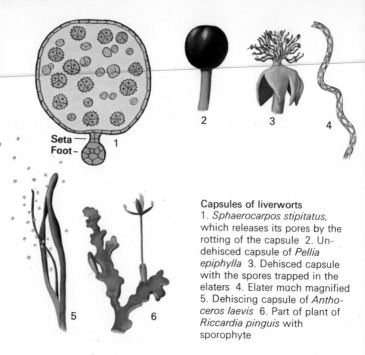

Capsules of liverworts
1. *Sphaerocarpos stipitatus,* which releases its pores by the rotting of the capsule 2. Undehisced capsule of *Pellia epiphylla* 3. Dehisced capsule with the spores trapped in the elaters 4. Elater much magnified 5. Dehiscing capsule of *Anthoceros laevis* 6. Part of plant of *Riccardia pinguis* with sporophyte

Seta
Foot

in the leaves. Each flask extends a mass of red hyphae and spores that are surrounded by nectar, which is the means of attracting insects to disperse the spores.

Apart from *Sphaerocarpos* and *Riccia,* where the spores are only liberated by decay of the capsule, the liverworts are aided in their spore dispersal by water-absorbing structures known as elaters. Each elater is a long narrow cell thickened by spiral bands. Elaters occur inside the capsules, either loosely mixed with the spores or attached to the capsule walls.

Marchantia has elaters free within the capsule, while those of *Riccardia* and *Pellia* are attached and organized into bundles. In *Pellia,* these bundles arise from the wall attached to the stalk, while in open *Riccardia* capsules the elaters are distributed as tufts on the tips of the four capsule segments.

An identical system occurs in the anthocerotes, where the loose elaters are exposed together with the spores as the mature tip of the capsule splits open. When the capsules split

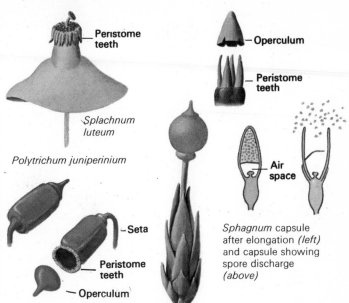

Capsules of mosses

Tetraphis pellucida

Peristome teeth

Operculum

Splachnum luteum

Peristome teeth

Polytrichum juniperinium

Air space

Seta

Peristome teeth

Operculum

Sphagnum capsule after elongation *(left)* and capsule showing spore discharge *(above)*

open, either along distinct stress lines or at random, the spores and their elaters are exposed to the atmosphere.

As the elaters dry out, the thickening bands cause the cells to twist, separating the spore mass and enabling the wind to disperse the spores individually. Such a mechanism probably helps to distribute the spores evenly to a wide variety of new sites, and therefore to spread the plant more effectively.

The use of water-sensitive mechanisms for spore dispersal is also found in the mosses. Here, however, the capsules rarely split open but allow their spores to escape from the top through special peristome teeth. When the lid at the top of the capsule is ejected, the peristome teeth are exposed. Like the elaters, they move as they absorb or lose water, closing the capsule when wet and opening it when dry. The relatively simple layout in the capsule of *Tetraphis* shows one layer of teeth, but that of *Funaria* has two layers which form an intricate mesh allowing the spores to escape only in small numbers.

Section of mature sporangium

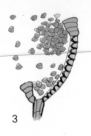

1 2 3

1. Annulus, a row of specialized elastic cells thickened on the innerside and containing water 2. As the ripe sporangium dries out the thin cells rupture 3. The annulus straightens 4. As the annulus bends back some of the spores are cast out. 5. The annulus recoils to close the sporangium, flinging the rest of the spores out, which may be carried further by air currents

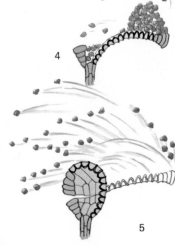

4

5

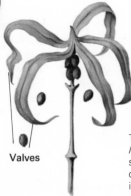

Valves

The capsule of Balsam, *Impatiens, (left)* ruptures suddenly under the tension caused by drying, thus scattering its seeds

The capsule of *Polytrichum* has refined dispersal to the stage where spores are actually sifted out in response to the wind. The structure of such capsules prevents spores from being blown out all at once; only strong winds will release the spores.

Dispersal in ferns is restricted to the asexual spores produced in the sporangia. The variety of sporangial types has been discussed, but in true ferns sporangia occur in groups on the leaf surface, often protected by a flap (indusium).

An ordinary fern sporangium, such as that of *Polystichum*, consists of a slender stalk and a bulbous chamber containing the spores. The sporangium wall has a row of thickened cells which stretch in a ridge from the stalk over the top to the other side, where the circle is completed by a number of thin-walled cells which mark the point of rupture. As the sporangium dries out, tensions set up within these cells are eventually great enough to disrupt the thin cells and allow the thickened cells to flick backwards like a tensed spring. As tension is released with the sporangium rupture, the wall recoils violently back to its original position, discharging the spores.

Dispersal in gymnosperms and angiosperms involves both pollen and seed. In the gymnosperms, the pollen is in many cases winged to assist wind dispersal, but among the angiosperms, which are mainly insect pollinated, adaptations to pollen dispersal are found in the sculpturing of the pollen coat. A rough coat enables the pollen to be attached to insects, while that of wind-pollinated species is usually smooth.

(Below) the underside of a single pinnule from a fern frond showing the sori and a mature sorus with half of the protecting indusium removed to reveal the stalked sporangia

Pine seeds

Sorus

Open cone of Mountain Pine

The seeds of gymnosperms are typically produced in cones. As the cone matures, and the seeds inside it ripen, it becomes woody and dies. Gradually the cone dries out and the scales part to reveal the seeds. Many pine cones, for example those of the Cedar, have winged seeds which may be carried by wind for some distance. Admittedly, there are over 200,000 different types of angiosperm, more than all other true plants put together, but the variety of dispersal devices used by the angiosperms is unequalled.

Among the explosive mechanisms, tensions due to drying of the fruit or a build-up of turgor pressure are the most important. The capsules of *Impatiens* species, notably the Jumping Jack or Policeman's Helmet, explode violently when ripe, scattering the seeds in all directions.

Gorse, Violet and Geranium fruits explode as a result of tensions caused by loss of water. The popping of Gorse pods on a hot day is a familiar example of this mechanism, whereby the black seeds are hurled for a distance of some feet. For the most part, however, angiosperm seeds or whole fruits are dispersed by means of water, wind or animals, and are adapted to this end. The Tumbleweed is an unusual adaptation to wind dispersal, where the whole plant becomes detached from its roots and rolls around in the wind, losing its seeds as it does so. The seeds themselves may be winged, as in *Bignonia* and the Sycamores, or have 'parachutes' of tiny hairs which catch the wind. Dandelions, Groundsels, Thistles and Fire-

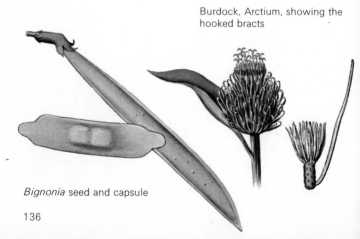

Burdock, Arctium, showing the hooked bracts

Bignonia seed and capsule

weeds are very common examples of seeds with 'parachutes'.

The term censer mechanism is applied to the capsule of Poppies, as the narrow slits usually present at the top of the ripe capsule allow the wind to sift the seeds out a few at a time; in this respect, there is a similarity with the capsules of the moss *Polytrichum*.

Other fruits may open by splitting into valves and exposing the seeds which are shaken or fall out. Still others may produce barbs on their surface which catch on passing animals. The Spanish Needle, Burdock and Cleavers are classic examples of this.

Oily seeds such as Gorse are often sought after by ants which may carry them for considerable distances, while the coloured flesh of some fruits attracts animals which digest them and release the seeds unharmed.

Distribution by water is found in a few instances. One amazing example is that of the Coconut, which may drift for hundreds of miles to new land. Water Lily seeds have a frill of buoyant tissus which enables them to be carried by streams to new sites, in common with the dispersal method of many aquatic plants.

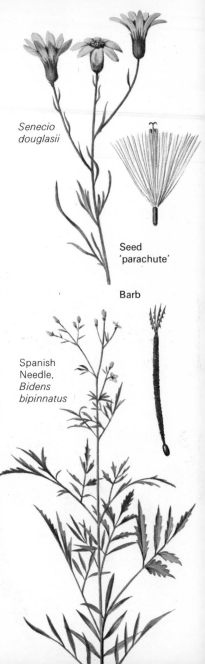

Senecio douglasii

Seed 'parachute'

Barb

Spanish Needle, *Bidens bipinnatus*

Birth

The spore, seed and other dispersal structures have several things in common: they are relatively small, specialized parts of the life-cycle which must be self-sufficient and able to survive perhaps long periods without food or water. The amount of food which they can contain depends partly on the way in which they are dispersed; a heavy seed cannot be successfully dispersed by wind. Yet when they have landed at a suitable spot they must be able to germinate and grow quickly once conditions are favourable.

What are these conditions? Obviously, they vary throughout the plant kingdom, but will include water, a suitable temperature and usually oxygen. Water is initially taken up by a sponge-like process which may take place very rapidly.

Initial growth will also depend on the food reserves present in the seed or spore until it has established contact with an exterior supply. This food reserve therefore has to maintain the plant slowly during dispersal, and rapidly during germination. If either dispersal or germination is excessively lengthy for a given seed, its chances of survival are accordingly reduced. This partly accounts for the enormous excess of seed or spore dispersal over the numbers of plants which become

Germination in bacteria; new cells grow out from the endospores of *Bacillus circulans*

Germination in a fungi; development of a new mycelium from a spore of *Gelasinospora calospora*

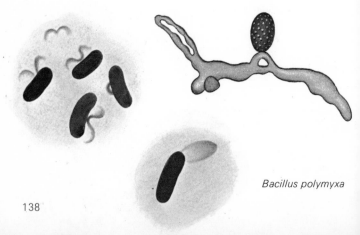

Bacillus polymyxa

Germinating spore
of the moss
Funaria develops
into a protonema,
bearing buds of
new moss plants

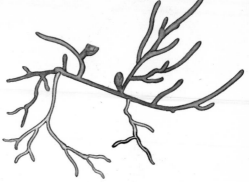

Germinating spore of the brown
alga *Sphacelaria cirrhosa*

established, one of the observations which led Darwin to
propose the *Theory of Natural Selection*. Certainly, natural
selection is most effective at this stage so that the dispersal
structures and their germination are critically related to the
life-cycle.

The lower plants produce unicellular spores which germinate to produce new organisms. The thick-walled spores of
bacteria and unicellular algae simply split to release new cells.
The resistant coat of the bacterial endospore loses its calcium
and other constituents as the spore begins to swell following
the uptake of water. Between half an hour and one hour later
the spore coat bursts open to release a young vegetative cell.

The spores of fungi usually germinate to produce a new
mycelium although the yeasts are among those in which the
spores start to multiply by budding. Myxomycete spores have
been known to germinate after sixty years in storage; they
release either motile 'swarm' cells, or produce a mycelium. A
surprising variety of treatments is sometimes required to
stimulate fungus spores to grow – including freezing, and
treatment with chemicals.

The spores of most pteridophytes are able to germinate
immediately on shedding, but probably rarely do. They are

Selaginella – female gametophyte develops within the spore

Ophioglossum will only develop beyond the 4-cell stage if infected by a fungus

Bothrodendron, a Pteridophyte fossil showing the gametophyte growing from the spore

able to develop into three types of gametophyte – the typical fern prothallus; a filamentous structure; or a very small gametophyte more or less enclosed by the spore. As a consequence, the germination and growth of the spore will vary according to the type of gametophyte that it will form.

The lycopods commonly produce some cells of the gametophyte within the spore before it has either germinated or been liberated. Rupture of the spore is accomplished by growth of the gametophyte. Spores of *Lycopodium* can live for three to eight years without germinating. The spores of the fossil *Bothrodendron*, another lycopod, germinated to produce a gametophyte which formed a small mass of cells projecting outside the ruptured walls.

In contrast, the pteridophyte spores which are green can only survive a few days

Marsilea – development of male gametophytes inside the microspore without germination, as in the case of *Equisetum*. The germinating spores of *Ophioglossum* will only survive beyond the production of three or four cells if they are invaded by a mycelial fungus, that will continue to live with the gametophyte through the rest of its life.

In all cases where an independent gametophyte is produced some of the first cells divide actively to form the thallus tissue, while one forms the rhizoids.

A section of a cycad seed shows the stony layer which encloses the developing embryo. This hard layer protects the embryo, enabling it to germinate even after two years, and is itself covered in a fleshy coat which is brightly coloured, usually red or orange.

Development of the embryo is continuous, although this cannot be seen from the outside. The seeds fall from the female branches of the plant, and lie on the ground. After some time, the coat cracks to reveal the root, which has forced its way through the stony layer. The cotyledons (commonly two) partly protrude, absorbing the gametophyte food store and passing it on to the seedling.

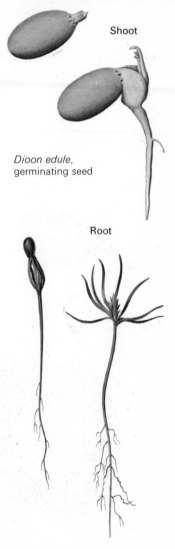

Shoot

Dioon edule, germinating seed

Root

Pinus seedlings showing the seed coat and numerous cotyledons surrounding the shoot

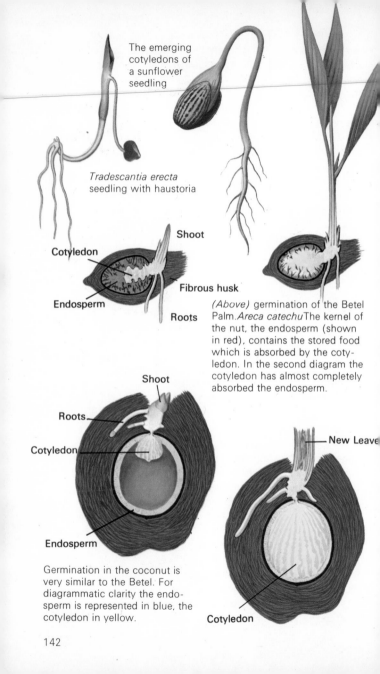

The emerging cotyledons of a sunflower seedling

Tradescantia erecta seedling with haustoria

Shoot

Cotyledon

Endosperm

Fibrous husk

Roots

(Above) germination of the Betel Palm.*Areca catechu* The kernel of the nut, the endosperm (shown in red), contains the stored food which is absorbed by the cotyledon. In the second diagram the cotyledon has almost completely absorbed the endosperm.

Shoot

Roots

Cotyledon

Endosperm

New Leaves

Cotyledon

Germination in the coconut is very similar to the Betel. For diagrammatic clarity the endosperm is represented in blue, the cotyledon in yellow.

Angiosperm seeds represent the most sophisticated dispersal units. According to the structure of the flower from which they are derived, they may be dispersed as seeds (Poppy, Laburnum) or as part of a fruit (Apple, Dandelion, Wheat, Coconut). This also affects their protection, rate of germination and whether they are buried in soil when they germinate.

The uptake (imbibition) of water is the first stage. Once this has occurred the seed must germinate. If the water supply then tails off, the seedlings will perish. Where this is likely to happen, for instance in arid regions, evolution has selected seeds which will only germinate when sufficient water is available to tide them over the germination period.

The coats of many seeds or fruits are very waxy or hard, and water uptake may only be stimulated by other factors. Some seed coats are so hard that they must be scraped before they will germinate, while others must be digested by animals. Some seeds exude mucilage once they have begun to absorb water, which increases the process and helps prevent drying out.

Germination must also take place at the right time of year for many seeds. Winter wheat requires exposure to cold before it will grow and therefore if sown in spring will refuse to germinate. Temperature and day-length are therefore important. Once germination has begun, however, the main shoot and root are pushed outside and begin to expand.

Often, the first leaves to appear are the cotyledons, but in many cases these remain underground within the seed. Where the cotyledon(s) appears above ground, it is green and can make food for the developing plant. The food within the seed is mobilized and absorbed in a variety of ways. Food may be stored in the cotyledon(s) or separately within the fruit.

An unusual example of food mobilization is seen in *Tradescantia erecta,* where a special absorbing structure penetrates the food reserve. The coconut *(Cocos nucifera)* has one of the largest supplies of food known in the angiosperms, and is therefore completely independent for some time. This is a feature common among the palms, which have a relatively slow germination. The Betel Palm *(Areca catechu)* illustrates the way in which the cotyledon grows into the food reserve, until, having absorbed it all, occupies the fruit completely.

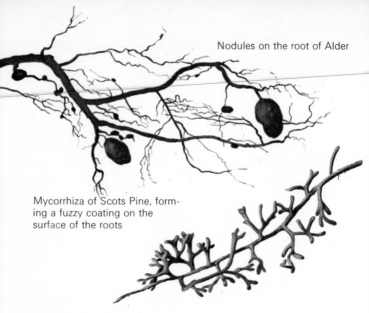

Nodules on the root of Alder

Mycorrhiza of Scots Pine, forming a fuzzy coating on the surface of the roots

Co-operation

Co-operation between plants and animals for their mutual benefit has already been seen in the cases of *Hydnophytum* and an *Acacia* species, where the plant is protected by ants in return for exuded sugar or shelter. These are quite clear examples. However, where two organisms are growing intertwined, as in lichens, it is often more difficult to determine whether only one partner benefits (parasitism) or both benefit equally (symbiosis).

In the case of lichens, one would expect the fungus to provide protection against water loss and to absorb minerals for the alga, which in return would donate some of the food it makes by photosynthesis to the fungus. While this is true to some extent, a number of cases are known where the fungal partner is parasitic on the alga.

Fungi also associate symbiotically with trees and other higher plants. The fungus forms an absorbing sheath (mycorrhiza) on the roots of trees, so that each partner donates nutrients which the other lacks. Most orchids have reached a stage where they are completely dependent on this mycorrhiza, and will not grow at all without it. In some cases, for example in the colourless *Corallorhiza,* the orchids are really parasitic on the mycorrhiza.

Plant roots are also surrounded by bacteria which help the plant to obtain its nutrients. This layer of bacteria is known as the rhizosphere. Leaf surfaces, too, harbour numerous organisms which may live in symbiosis with the plant. Bacteria also occur inside the roots (as nodules), in the growing points of the shoots, or in seeds. Of these associations, the nitrogen-fixing nodules of legumes (such as Pea, Lupin, Beans) are the best understood. These nodules harbour nitrogen-fixing bacteria which receive food in return for supplying the plant with nitrogen compounds. Such nodules also occur on many other plants, including the Alder, Buckthorn and *Casuarina,* although it is not absolutely certain in these cases whether the fixation of nitrogen is due to bacteria or other organisms.

Dispersal is obviously a field of co-operation between organisms. Where pollen or nectar are attractive to animals (particularly insects) both the plant and animal benefit. The animal can, of course, be deceived into

Corallorhiza innata, a colourless orchid that depends entirely on its mycorrhiza for food.

Mycorrhiza on the reduced rooting system.

thinking that it has found something desirable; the example of the Cuckoo-pint producing a foetid smell which attracts insects, thinking they have at last found some decaying flesh, has already been quoted. Similarly, the spores of the fungus *Phallus* and its allies are dispersed in the same way, while the mosses of the Splachnaceae family also rely on this mechanism.

Among higher plants, *Stapelia* attracts carrion flies which commonly lay their eggs in the flower, believing they have found a suitable source of food for their offspring. In this way, quite accidentally, the flower is pollinated. However, there are numerous examples of more specialized relationships between flowers and pollinating insects.

The flowers of the *Yucca (left)* are pollinated by the moth, *Tegiticula yuccasella*, which lays its eggs in the ovaries. *(Bottom right)* a seed pod with holes through which the larvae have emerged.

The Carrion Flower, *Stapelia grandiflora*, is visited by flies attracted by the foetid smell.

The Heather, *Calluna,* produces a ring of nectar at the base of the ovary, partly enclosed by the stamens. The female of the insect *Taeniothrips* inevitably dislodges pollen on to itself in its frantic probing for the nectar and carries it to the styles of the flowers as it takes off or lands in its search for the flightless male. Eggs are laid in the petals, which are partly eaten by the emerging grubs before they pupate in the soil.

Yucca is pollinated by *Tegiticula yuccasella* in a more deliberate way. Pollen is gathered up and conveyed to the styles before eggs are laid in the ovary. When the eggs hatch, the larvae live comfortably on some of the ovules before they leave the flower. Pollination of the flower is therefore ensured, although some of the seeds are eaten and the insect benefits as well. A similar situation exists in *Trollius,* a buttercup relative, where eggs of *Chiastochaeta trolli* are laid in the base of the ovary. Pollination is completely accidental, as the insects tramp freely about the flowers.

Interference

Plants interfere with one anothers' growth. Tall trees shade the plants growing beneath them, often blotting out most of the light, while competition for nutrients, light and water cause densely-sown seedlings to be much smaller than those which are thinly-sown. Interference, or competition, is therefore a result of the fact that any given environment has only a limited amount of resources. As it can only support a certain amount of life, plants are consequently in competition for these resources and interfere with each other as a result.

To these facts must be added the possibility of a sudden shortage or even excess of any of the resources – the habitat can flood or dry up, it can suffer high levels of sunlight; nutrients or even soil can be washed away, to mention only some. And it is always, if subtly, changing. It is therefore not surprising that plants must be adapted to interference as well as to the normal functions of their life-cycle. In fact, the two go hand-in-hand in an eternal cycle of cause and effect.

No single species can make use of all the range of environmental resources simultaneously, and this leads to divergence of plants for different requirements. It has been experimentally shown that if two very similar species are put in direct competition for the same habitat they will change, as a result of selection over several generations, to have different requirements. Hence interference results in either divergence or extinction. On this simple basis it can perhaps be seen that such processes are responsible for the variety of ways in which different plants solve the same problems that have been discussed in previous chapters of this book. For this reason, too, plants tend to be associated in communities which to some extent contain species that are compatible; if they were not, one

The sequence from left to right illustrates how a patch of bare earth may be colonized by a succession of plants.

Regeneration of heather 1.
Mature plant, a small compact
clump 2. A senescent plant
where the centre dies back and
is invaded by lichens 3. The tips
of the shoots root again forming
young clumps beginning the
cycle once more.

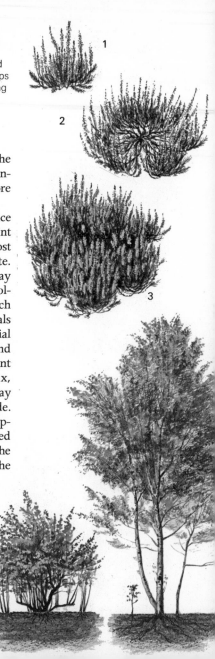

would 'swamp' another. The flora of a heath, marsh, mountain or sea-shore is therefore to some extent predictable.

The effect of interference on the development of a plant community can be seen most clearly on a bonfire site. Firstly, some mosses may germinate and flourish, followed by small weeds such as annual grasses. The annuals are followed by perennial herbs and then by shrubs and tree seedlings. Development eventually reaches a climax, which if upset in any way may allow new species to invade.

Each successive development in the cycle is caused partly by the fact that the colonizers may change the

The top leaves of *Ficus* grow horizontally, while those below slope increasingly to catch maximum light.

environment to their detriment, and also by the ability of many slower-growing species to dominate the smaller, quick-growing ones. Such a process is known as succession.

On a small scale, succession can be seen on heaths where Heather *(Calluna)* or Bracken *(Pteridium)* predominate. As the Heather plant expands its tuft the centre often becomes bare, allowing other plants, notably lichens, to colonize the space. The edges of the clump eventually form separate plants by rooting, and begin the process over again. Dieback in the older parts of *Pteridium* systems releases a great deal of potassium to the poor soil, encouraging the growth of grasses and other weeds, particularly a species of Bedstraw.

The resources which plants compete for are usually light,

The African Violet, *Saintpaulia*, creates a rosette of leaves, the inner having short stalks and the outer long stalks.

water and nutrients. Of these, any one may be limiting. This effect on plant growth is rather like the speed of traffic on a busy road being limited by that of the slowest vehicle. Light is often the limiting factor. The close cover of a thriving crop will prevent the smaller weeds from reaching the light, and kill them as effectively as leaving a box on a lawn for a long time would kill the grass.

Where the plants are tall and the foliage is mainly at the top of the stem, sufficient light may reach the lower plants from the side. Such a situation exists in many woods. The usual pattern, however, is that the trees form an effective mosaic of leaves which do not interfere with each other and still allow some light to reach the floor of the wood. Individual plants therefore often have a system which prevents their own leaves from interfering with each other.

Among the many striking examples of this feature perhaps one of the clearest is that of a *Ficus* species. The uppermost leaves are horizontal, and present the greatest surface area to

Tree roots take up most of the moisture from the surrounding area *(above)* but if an area is trenched off, a wide variety of plant life may be established.

The Brittle-bush, *Encelia farinosa*, has the capacity to produce a toxin preventing the growth of other plants.

the light. These large leaves would therefore overshadow the lower ones, were it not that they are successively inclined down the stem towards the vertical in order to trap light. A similar adaptation is seen in *Saintpaulia,* where the older leaves have longer stalks that carry them away from the younger leaves to prevent overcrowding and present a rosette of leaves to the light.

The growth of Rhubarb in spring also demonstrates how the leaves increase the length of their stalks until the plant presents a very large surface area; grown as a crop they completely dominate the area they cover without interfering greatly with each other. Quite commonly, water is not a limiting factor, but in a forest the effect of competition for water may be quite marked. Around the bases of the trees the soil may be quite dry, and support little plant life except mosses. If a section is trenched off to kill the roots within it, a surprising variety of plant life may establish itself, showing how effectively trees can take up the available water. Soil is not a limiting factor, unless one considers nutrient resources, as it can take any number of rooting systems if sufficient water is available.

Competition achieves by natural means what man achieves artificially – the plant best suited to the environment. Under natural conditions these conditions may cover the whole range of the plant's activities. In other words, plants have diversified in a wide variety of ways to fulfil essentially the same functions such as breeding dispersal and feeding. Man, however, selects useful plants for particular requirements – yield of fruit, leaves, colour of flowers and so on. With the advent of mechanical farming, plants are being bred to make the job easier and to give higher yields. The use of tomato-picking machines, for example, has required the breeding of specially-shaped tomatoes.

This tailoring of the plant to certain requirements is sometimes made possible by crossing a wide variety of related

Walnut also contains chemicals which prevent the growth of other plants. In this illustration Walnut extract is used to show this effect on the growth of tomato plants.

Walnut extract

No extract

species to bring together in one plant the required characteristics. For instance, an improved strain of wheat may have a stronger or shorter stem for withstanding wind, but have no resistance for certain diseases. This has to be bred in from other strains of the same species or even from different species. The proportions of a plant can now be altered to suit production of fruits only; within a few decades crop plants may be scarcely recognizable as having originated from wild species.

Divergence is a feature of evolution – man is merely speeding up the process deliberately. The same principle applies to chemicals, so that certain plants may be selected to yield very high levels of one particular useful compound, or the balance of chemicals may be altered so that the oils they produce are more palatable to the human taste. The improvement of margarine is one example of this. 'Nature invented it first', is a saying used to describe the copying of principles found in nature for man's use. And of course one cannot do this without first knowing something about the diversity of Nature. Certainly, the fascinating range of structures and

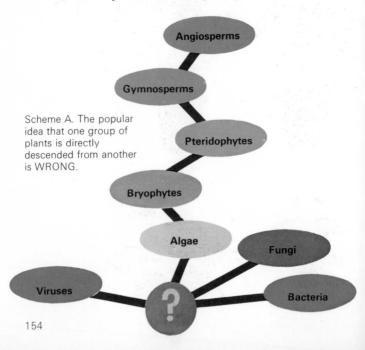

Scheme A. The popular idea that one group of plants is directly descended from another is WRONG.

mechanisms that are found throughout the plant kingdom are well worth studying. As a final footnote, it must be emphasized that the sequence of plants described in this book is not necessarily the order of their evolution. Far from it: the angiosperms are not directly related to the gymnosperms, nor the gymnosperms to the pteridophytes, and so on.

Such major higher groups are currently believed to have arisen within a short time of each other when plants first colonized land. Nevertheless, the trend of reduction of the gametophyte among plants which successfully diverged to meet the demands of an erratic, often dry, environment is still significant. Admittedly many fossil plants can be quoted as being identical with living specimens, indicating that they have remained stationary, but this does not necessarily imply that the lower groups have remained static. On the contrary, many lower plants are surprisingly adaptable and plastic. There is an unfortunate tendency to regard the lower plants as being inferior to the higher ones. This is not really true, as it is hoped this book has shown.

Scheme B. This shows how they are probably related.

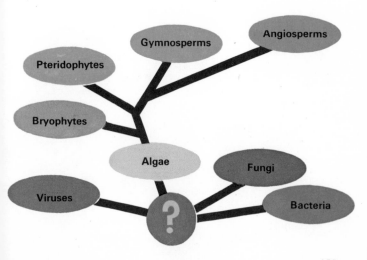

BOOKS TO READ

An Evolutionary Survey of the Plant Kingdom by R. F. Scagel et al. Blackie, London, 1967.

British Mosses and Liverworts by E. V. Watson. Second edition, Cambridge University Press, 1968.

British Wild Flowers by J. Hutchinson. Pelican A331, 1955.

Ferns, Mosses and Fungi. A Little Guide in Colour, Paul Hamlyn, 1969.

Foundations of Modern Biology Series. Prentice Hall, New Jersey.

General Microbiology by Stanier, Doudoroff & Adelberg. Macmillan, London, 1963.

Observer's Book of Mosses and Liverworts. Frederick Warne, London, 1964.

Plants Variation and Classification by C. Bell. Fundamentals of Botany Series, Wadsworth, California, 1967.

The Advance of the Fungi by E. C. Large. Jonathan Cape, London, 1958.

The Evolution of Life by F. H. T. Rhodes. Pelican A512, 1963.

The Growth of Plants by G. E. Fogg. Pelican A560, 1963.

The Life of Plants by E. J. H. Corner. Weidenfeld & Nicholson, London, 1964.

The Natural History of Europe by Harry Garms. Paul Hamlyn, London, 1967.

INDEX

SOME OTHER TITLES IN THIS SERIES

Natural History

The Animal Kingdom
Australian Animals
Bird Behaviour
Birds of Prey
Fishes of the World
Fossil Man
A Guide to the Seashore

Life in the Sea
Mammals of the World
Natural History Collecting
Prehistoric Animals
Snakes of the World
Wild Cats

Gardening

Chrysanthemums
Garden Flowers

Garden Shrubs
Roses

Popular Science

Atomic Energy
Computers at Work
Electronics

Mathematics
Microscopes & Microscopic Life
The Weather Guide

Arts

Architecture
Jewellery

Porcelain
Victoriana

General Information

Flags
Military Uniforms
Rockets & Missiles
Sailing

Sailing Ships & Sailing Craft
Sea Fishing
Trains

Domestic Animals & Pets

Budgerigars
Cats
Dogs

Horses & Ponies
Pets for Children

Domestic Science

Flower Arranging

History & Mythology

Discovery of
   Africa
   The American West
   Japan
   North America

Myths & Legends of
   Ancient Egypt
   Ancient Greece
   The South Seas